PP 45-48
missing

BELA LUGOSI

MASTER OF THE MACABRE

BELA LUGOSI

MASTER OF THE MACABRE

LARRY EDWARDS

McGuinn & McGuire
PUBLISHING, INC.
Bradenton, Florida

"BORIS KARLOFF" PAGE 635 from THE FILM ENCYCLOPEDIA by EPHRAIM KATZ. Copyright © 1979 by Ephraim Katz & See Hear Productions, Inc. Reprinted by permission of HarperCollins Publishers, Inc.

From THE FILMS OF BELA LUGOSI by Richard Bojarski. Copyright © 1980 by Richard Bojarski. Published by arrangement with Carol Publishing Group. A Citadel Press Book.

Excerpts from pages 128, 129, 611, 984, 1305 from HALLIWELL'S FILM GUIDE, 1994 EDITION by LESLIE HALLIWELL. Copyright © 1993, 1992, 1991 by Ruth Halliwell and John Walker. Copyright © 1989, 1987, 1983, 1981, 1979, 1977 by Leslie Halliwell. Reprinted by permission of HarperCollins Publishers, Inc.

Excerpts from "Hollywood Gothic" by David Skal, copyright © 1990 by David J. Skal. Reprinted with permission of W.W. Norton Company.

Library of Congress Cataloging-in-Publication Data

Edwards, Larry, 1957-
    Bela Lugosi: master of the macabre / Larry Edwards.
       p.   cm.
    Includes bibliographical references and index.
    ISBN 1-881117-09-X (alk. paper)
      1. Lugosi, Bela, 1882-1956. 2. Actors – Hungary – Biography.
   3. Motion picture actors and actresses – United States – Biography.
    I. Title.
    PN2859.H86L834   1995
    791.43'028'092 – dc20
    [b]   95-33369

DEDICATION

When I was a child, I had an obsession with going to the movies on Saturdays. It was an illness – I had to go! To my recollection, there never was a time when my parents said, "No" to this weekly ritual (and they never asked what the film was rated). Because of this, my love of the cinema has become one of my careers. So, this book is dedicated to my mother and father.

To my son Mathew, you are proof that miracles don't just happen in the movies!

To Christopher Carroll and the staff at McGuinn & McGuire Publishing, Inc.: Thank you for the confidence and the kind words.

And of course, to the memory of Bela Lugosi. May your reign as the Master of the Macabre last until the final person on earth has shuddered at your art.

CONTENTS

BORN TO BE DRACULA   1

AMERICA, THE BEAUTIFUL   23

DRACULA: THE MAKING OF A LEGEND   43

BELA AND BORIS: A DEADLY DUO!   81

MADNESS, MAYHEM, AND THE MACABRE   107

FALLING FROM GRACE   129

THE FINAL BOW   153

STAGEOGRAPHY   165

FILMOGRAPHY   175

BIBLIOGRAPHY   193

APPENDIX A   195

APPENDIX B   205

INDEX   207

In all the annals of living horror, one name stands out as the epitome of evil: Dracula!

The very mention of the name brings to mind things so evil, so fantastic, so degrading, that you wonder if it all isn't just a dream – a nightmare.

This is no dream . . .

This is DRACULA!

CHAPTER ONE

BORN TO BE DRACULA

As you climb the curvy, rocky roads leading up the Carpathian Mountains in Romania, the stench of death permeates your nostrils. In every direction, the sickening, caustic scent of blood hangs in the air almost like the fog which envelops San Francisco nightly. It is this area of the fabled Carpathian Mountains where the "Terror of Transylvania" roamed and killed at will, leaving his castle and venturing into the countryside to wreak his deadly havoc in a most ghastly and gruesome manner.

The "Terror of Transylvania," Vlad Dracula (1431–1476), nicknamed "Vlad the Impaler," is still a Romanian folklore legend and one of the main reasons why tourists make side trips to his castle in Hungary. (Transylvania, now a part of Hungary, was in Romania during the reign of Dracula.) This legend of murder has made it a tourist trap in this part of the world.

When it comes to murder, madness, and mayhem, Vlad Dracula may be one of the most accomplished murderers in world history. On any given night, Dracula and his army would venture into various towns and commit acts of wanton murder. A few examples:

The merchants in one small town balked at paying "taxes." In response, Dracula road into the town with his army and murdered every merchant. His victims were impaled on steel stakes and left in a "picket fence" pattern around the town to display his murderous power.

After invading a small hamlet of peasants, Dracula had his army create special cauldrons. Once the cauldrons were constructed, the peasants were boiled alive. As they were being boiled, their heads remained

1

visible; Dracula wanted to watch them in agony and wanted the surrounding towns and hamlets to hear their screams. While watching this most gruesome mass murder, Dracula feasted on the peasants' pets.

When a tour of 41 German teenagers ventured to Romania to study the language, Dracula thought they were sent to spy on him. With his paranoia running rampant, he ordered each of the teenagers to be impaled lengthwise and alive.

After hearing that a few citizens of a town named Brasov were cursing his name, Vlad Dracula led his army into the town to commit unimaginable atrocities. Each citizen of Brasov (men, women, and children) was impaled, both crosswise and lengthwise, and while they were still alive, Dracula's army dismembered them. The blood of these innocent citizens of Brasov was then gathered into clay casks so that Dracula and his army could dip their bread in it before they supped.

To show his utter disdain of Germans, Dracula ordered as many Germans as possible to be brought before him. On August 24, 1460, at least 30,000 Germans living in Romania were herded into the Carpathian Mountains, at the foothills of Castle Dracula. Then, like an orchestra conductor leading a symphony of death, he ordered all 30,000 to be killed. Most were impaled and all were decapitated. By the week's end, impaled bodies lined the path leading to Castle Dracula and human heads on stakes dotted the acreage surrounding the castle.

A few centuries after the deadly reign of Vlad Dracula, Bela Blasko was born (October 20, 1882), in a small village called Lugos, in the shadows of the Carpathian Mountains and within sight of Castle Dracula. Born on the same soil , which was once soaked with the blood of the innocent victims of the "real" Dracula, seemed almost prophetic. A few decades after his birth, Bela Blasko won world acclaim for his portrayal of the fictional Dracula. It is easy to imagine that Bela Blasko was "born to be Dracula!"

To understand the adolescence of Bela Blasko more fully, it is important to first understand the times of the region where he grew up. Lugos, Hungary was an area which was constantly in political turmoil (much like it has been in recent years). At any time, during any particular year, troops invaded Hungary from the surrounding countries and patrolled the streets of Lugos. Stability and complacency were neither physical nor mental aspects of living in this area. Nightmares were common to the children who lived in that region. At this particular time, the fabled name of Vlad Dracula was rarely uttered by a Hungarian because it disgusted most citizens. He was not then the folklore legend he is today (thanks to Hollywood in general and Bela Lugosi in particular).

Lugos, Hungary, in the late 1800's, was a stereotypical mid-European hamlet. When horse-drawn carriages trod upon the century-old stone roads, they created miniature dust storms. Most of the houses in town were made of stone and built side-by-side, one atop the other. Outside of the town, the situation was quite different. Squatter camps, traveling communities of middle-European gypsies who reveled in the occult and dabbled in assortments of Old World ceremonies, ritual and rites were rampant throughout the miles of farmlands

Often, the young Bela ventured out to one of the gypsy encampments. Hidden behind a grove of trees or clumps of rocks, he hypnotically gazed at these families. Later in his life, in the movie *The Wolf Man*, he played a gypsy (a small but extremely powerful characterization) and used the mystique of the gypsies he had watched as a youth .

The Blasko family was not monetarily well-off, by any stretch of the imagination; however, they were not paupers, either. According to to-day's standards, they were "middle class." This is contrary to the Universal Pictures' press release of the film *Dracula*. The studio stated, "Lugosi's father was a Baron descended from a Nobleman who earned vast land holdings surrounding his native land of Lugos." Universal Pictures inferred that Bela was indeed a descendant of Count Dracula.

The Blasko family reflected any typical European family of this era. The father, Istvan, ruled his domestic domain, which included: Bela's mother Paula (Vojnits), his brother Ludovious, and his two sisters, Joanna and Vilma. Istvan, who came from a family of farmers, often looked tradition in the face only to spit upon it; he was a rebel before the word had meaning. Bela inherited this rebellious trait from his father. Istvan turned away from the family's tradition of farming and opted for the business life of a banker for the town of Lugos (not at all the prestigious position, that it may sound).

As the typical "king of his castle," Istvan ruled his family with an iron fist. He was a methodical, immaculate, demanding, perfectionist who would not stand for anything short of absolute respect from his family. He never laid a hand on either his wife or his children in anger. The type of punishment he would mete out was psychological in nature. In an inter-view with Bela, shortly after achieving star status in America, Bela stated that his father was a strict disciplinarian. Once, when he was late for dinner, his father admonished Bela and made him sit at the table without food, while other members of the family ate their dinners.

Any historian will quickly point out that growing up in this area of Europe, during the late 1800's, was a political nightmare brought to life. Hungary was a mixture of cultures, nationalities and religions. Sometimes, when the adults weren't fighting their politicized confrontations with words, they used weapons. The youths Bela's age also had their own battles to fight – gang rivalry or turf wars – much like what was going on in the inner cities of America in the 1990's.

Famed Hollywood film producer, Joseph Pasternak, grew up in the same region of Hungary as Bela. Pasternak once said that growing up in this era was confusing because, although he and Bela had Hungarian sympathies, they were neither Hungarian or Romanian. He said that, in school, Romanian teachers would discriminate against Hungarian students, so they tried to conceal their views. When he made this statement, he was not aware of Bela's "closeted" activities, the leader of a Hungarian youth gang.

Youth gangs, at the turn-of-the-century Europe, were commonplace, but, in a country such as Hungary with its continual political uprisings, they were almost a necessity for a teen to survive. Because of Bela's rebellious ways, it seemed natural for him to be a gang leader. Not only was Bela a gang leader, by gang standards, he was almost infamous.

Like today's gangs, the gangs of Bela's time and locale were formed according to nationality. The two largest gangs were the Romanians and the Hungarians – Bela was, obviously, a leader of one of the Hungarian gangs.

Like the youth gangs of America in the 1990's, the youth gangs of Bela's era had leaders which led factions of their respective gang. Bela was the leader of the "scalpers." Previous writings on Bela Lugosi would have the reader believe that, like some American Indians, the scalpers actually took the scalp of their rivals. Though it makes for some particularly gruesome stories, this was not the case. How these rumors got started is anyone's guess. Bela was only ten years old at the time.

Regarding his days as a scalper, Bela said the following:

> One of my most passionate pursuits was the acquiring of scalps! That is, we pretended they were scalps. In our town, we were half Romanians and half Hungarians. There were two schools, one for the Hungarians, the other for the Romanians.

Figure 1 – Bela, as Dracula, getting ready to sink his teeth into the role. One eye is lit and the other is in the shadow. This lighting mistake occurred throughout the film and soon became known as the "Bela Logo." (Copyright © 1931 by Universal Studios, Inc. Courtesy of MCA Publishing Rights, a Division of MCA Inc. All Rights Reserved)

To show the superiority of the Hungarians, it was our habit to take hats away from the Romanian boys, pretending they were scalps we took, like the American Indians. I had, at one time, seven hundred hats of Romanian boys! I gloated over them. They showed my superiority and leadership.

And what did the young Bela Lugosi do with all of the "scalps" he collected? He sold them. "I made a lot of money!"

It is erroneous to assume that this gang activity was "just a bunch of adolescent boys burning off innocent energy." Gang fights usually resulted from these scalpings, often with serious results. On more than a few occasions, the outcome for some gang members was death.

Although he was actively involved in gang activity, most likely because of peer pressure, his mind and his focus was on the theater. Bela's formal education consisted of only a few years of elementary school at the Superior Hungarian State Gymnasium (the local institute of public education). There's a simple reason why his educational training lasted only a few years – he just wasn't interested in school. So, he dropped out at the age of 11.

Bela's quitting school dismayed his family; they were disgusted with him. A child's education was of paramount importance to the Blasko family. A youth did not simply elect to quit school. Bela had brought shame upon his family. It was something Istevan could not take.

When he quit school, Bela decided to pursue his real interest, acting. It actually started when a traveling troupe of actors ventured through Logos. This group of Romanian gypsies traveled from town to town and performed dramatizations created by Hungarian and Romanian playwrights. After sneaking into one of their performances, Bela was bitten by the acting bug.

In reference to Bela's early years of acting, a 1935 press release about his film (serial) *The Return of Chandu*, read, in part:

In Hungary, acting is a career for which one fits himself as earnestly and studiously as one studies for a degree in medicine, law or philosophy. In Hungary, acting is a profession. In America, it is a decision. A youth "decides" he will go on the stage or appear in pictures. If the public accepts him, the "decision" automatically becomes final.

Mind you, this attributed quote is not Bela's, but a film studio's and, as studios are known to do (then and now), they exaggerate to the point of blatant lying. In fact, acting in the Hungary of Bela's youth was not on a par with becoming a doctor, lawyer or philosopher. As a matter of fact, acting as a career was thought of as being a low career choice, although it did present quite a profitable opportunity for the producers of these dramatic performances.

An amazing anecdote follows the Bela Lugosi legend. It is believed by some that he achieved his first acting job at age 11 when playing the male lead in William Shakespeare's tragic romance, *Romeo and Juliet*. Once again, this is not a fact, but the result of a studio's publicity department. This rumor started in the *Philadelphia Public Ledger*, August 13, 1933. It read:

> A theatrical troupe in *Romeo and Juliet* was billed to play in the small province in which Lugosi lived. Of the population, none was more interested in the forthcoming event than the young Lugosi.
>
> During the afternoon previous to the scheduled performance of the play, an unexpected bit of news exploded in the rumor channels. Romeo had been taken ill suddenly and it might be necessary to change the program for the evening. To avert this change, the young Lugosi was drafted to play the part.

An accurate publicity ploy would have been written like the following: In 1893, at the age of 11, Bela Lasko (Lugosi), received his first taste of acting. After sneaking into numerous performances of the aforementioned traveling troupe of actors, Bela made a decision; a decision which would change his life. He quit school to pursue the art of acting.

Once Bela decided go into acting, he had a fight on his hands – though this time it had nothing to do with youth gangs. This fight was with his father, a man who was as "bullheaded" as the young Bela. When Istvan laid down the law, he said that Bela must attend the national academy of higher learning (high school). Bela rebelled by doing the unexpected – he ran away from home. A truly courageous escapade for a young boy of 11 (especially considering the political turmoil of his Motherland at the time).

Bela ran away to Resita, a mining town just a little more than 300 miles south of Lugos, Hungary. With what little money he had saved from peddling his "scalps" from his gang days, Bela purchased transportation (train and horse-drawn coach); but, most of his trip was traveled by foot. Once he finally arrived in Resita, he found his older sister Vilma and moved in with her. Then, with his heart set on acting career, he investigated the many theatrical avenues Resita had to offer. Because of his young age, lack of experience and immaturity, his ventures went unnoticed. With this lack of interest in his talents, Bela was not dissuaded, though he was disheartened.

Needing money to survive (not to mention proving to his father that he was not a "loser in life"), Bela became a laborer working in a mine. When Bela spoke of these hard times, he said that he first worked as an apprentice in the mine. It was there, in the dark bowels of the earth, that he sometimes thought that he might go mad. It was there that he recognized his fear of the darkness, a darkness he associated with another world.

Working the mines not only gave Bela his "learning of horror," it also contributed to his distaste of yelling. Yelling was necessary to be heard in the mines. This aversion spilled over into his acting; he was one of the few actors in the horror cinema who rarely raised his voice to frighten the theater-goers. When he wasn't laboring in the mines of Resita, Bela continued his struggle to break into acting. He had a few nibbles, walk-on parts and "human" backgrounds, but Bela's ego was too large for him to accept these minor pieces. (It was this same ego problem that caused him, years later, to forego the chance to play Frankenstein's monster in the Universal film, *Frankenstein*).

After several months of breathing gaseous fumes in the mines and receiving numerous dramatic nibbles, Bela was finally offered a speaking role in a play (and the opportunity to get noticed). While basking in his egotistical glow, personal tragedy struck. During preparation for his first "real" appearance on the Hungarian stage, Bela was shocked back into reality when he was told of his father's death. This was Bela's first personal encounter with death. Because Istvan had been in good health, the shock hit especially hard. According to information reported to Bela, Istvan came home from work at his bank and, as punctual as usual, sat down to dinner. After being served soup, he positioned the spoon in its rightful spot, neatly folded his napkin, looked at his wife (Paula) and then fell over dead.

Though Bela and Istvan were somewhat estranged, the bond between them was more solid than most father and son relationships. Bela knew that he had received his inner strength from his father. This inner strength that they shared was the source of their constant disagreements. Bela then understood why he pursued his acting goals with such persistence. He felt indebted to his father and he felt pangs of guilt because he had never expressed that love and respect to his father. Bela's guilt and sadness consumed him. His dream of becoming a great actor temporarily was set aside.

Bela's melancholy worried his sister Vilma. She decided it was time to step in and play her part of "big sister." She used what limited influence she had with a small theatrical group based in Resita to get him a job as one of the troupe's chorus boys. The boy who was to become Bela Lugosi, Master of the Macabre, actually got his first break in show business as a chorus boy. Troupe members were dismayed, to put it lightly, to discover his lack of acting ability.

Bela then realized how ignorant he was because of his poor education. He could not read or write so he became known as the troupe's in-house "mute" – "mute" because all he was able to do was stand on the stage and look pretty. (He mouthed what he thought were the words to the songs the other chorus boys sang). Because he was illiterate, people continually made fun of Bela. Their mean-spirited ridicule often pushed him to uncontrollable tears. Because of this, Bela learned two lessons: he must better himself through education and, though it took longer to achieve, he must learn to please himself before he could even attempt to please others.

Bela recalls his bittersweet days with the acting troupe from Resita:

> I was so awkward. They tried to give me little parts in their plays, but I was so uneducated, so stupid, people just laughed at me. But I got the taste of the stage. I got, also, the rancid taste of humiliation. It was then, too, that I got the knowledge of the main key to my character . . . that I had the ability to focus my will, my mind, my body, my emotions in to one deep and driving channel.

In an effort to better himself, Bela conducted a self-taught crash-course in reading (necessary for an aspiring actor to acquire). "For ten years, day and night, night and day, with only one, two, three hours of sleep, I read and read and read until I could talk with any college professor in the world." Bela was not exaggerating, by the time he came to America, he was not only regarded as one of Europe's finest actors, but one of its most intellectual, as well.

American studios, which had Bela under contract until 1943, never knew that he was once ignorant. During an interview, he let the news slip out:

> For purposes of publicity, for the purpose of simplification, I have always thought it better to tell a lie about the early years of my life. It is the madness of the young, perhaps, to tell boasting lies without maturity of mind to recognize that to tell the truth is sometimes truer boasting.

(It is interesting to note that after this interview ran in newspapers nationally, the career of Bela Lugosi began its horrific decline.)

It is logical to assume that during Bela's early days on the Hungarian stage, he was not known as Bela Lugosi. However, assumptions should never be made about the legendary Bela Lugosi. Because he was a runaway, Bela changed his name from Bela Blasko to Bela Lugosi. On the way to his now famous name, Bela also assumed the identities of Geeza Lugosi and Dezso Lugosi before settling on Bela Lugosi, the surname meaning "originating from Lugos."

Once Bela began to learn to read and write, the Resita troupe offered him more parts. Most of the dramatizations were written and performed by members of the troupe. It was not as emotionally draining as Shakespeare, which gave Bela the chance to relay emotions to the audience. This greatly enhanced his self-esteem.

With an improved self-image, Bela's acting abilities were noticed by the drama critics who covered the various hamlets, townships, and cities surrounding Resita. Bela recognized that it was time to move on to bigger and betters venues. He left the Resita troupe to join an unnamed troupe which traveled Hungary and played in anything from tents to grand opera houses. Bela was learning his artistic craft in spades as a member of this new troupe. Aside from performing many Hungarian-written plays, he was also getting a shot at the classics and, in some cases, operettas. While performing in these operettas, Bela perfected his strong baritone – the same baritone which has echoed one of the cinema's greatest opening lines: "I am Dracula!" It was also his rich baritone which garnered him critical notice and rave reviews when he performed *Dracula* on Broadway during the late 1920's (before the film).

Because this traveling troupe performed as many as three different plays per week, Bela had to memorize as many as 40 roles per year and keep each one polished as the troupe would decide which production to perform the day of the performance. One of the strangest roles Bela played during this time was that of Jesus Christ, strange because it was Bela portraying Christ – the man who epitomized satanic virtues on film was the holiest of the holy on the European stage.

Bela's first taste of a character in the horror genre came in 1903. This was the first time two of Bela's most notable cinematic traits were cast upon the entertainment public: his dark, hypnotic eyes and the ballet-type gracefulness with which he could glide through scenes. The play was *Trilby*, written by Svengali. Bela portrayed Gecko and the reviewers raved. Though this was Bela's first taste of horror, the European theatrical community was not ready to typecast him (typecasting being an American habit). The roles which would follow Bela's portrayal of Gecko in *Trilby* were the opposite of horror, they were romantic roles; roles which led American critics writing about the entertainment scene in Europe to dub him "Europe's most romantic stage actor."

Because of Bela's penchant for romantic roles and his uncanny ability to project an aura of erotica, he was becoming not just one of Hungary and Europe's most popular actors. He was also becoming one of the first "sex symbols" to grace the European boards. Like the sex symbols of today's cinematic generation, he was also receiving large amounts of mail – marriage proposals and countless invitations for sex. As Bela was becoming the matinee idol of his time and region, the drama critics were also becoming enamored by his talents. As one critic in Szeged wrote: "The pleasant, handsome actor will certainly become one of the greats, judging by the audience reaction to his performances." Other critics were not so kind in their reviews when they wrote of Bela's aura of romanticism. One critic from Budapest noted:

> Why the young actor feels it important to strut and glance as he does, is unknown, but surely it inhibits what little ability he possesses . . . . So enamored is he in himself, that if he were to portray Iago, he would make Shakespeare wince in pain as his ogre character would be portrayed as a lustful lecher.

With all the notoriety he was receiving for his acting abilities, Bela felt it was time to move on; time to better himself and make his name synonymous with the European stage. It was at this point in Bela's life that historians believe he joined the Academy of Theatrical Arts. This belief is understandable because Bela not only talked about his tenure with this theater, one of the best in Europe, but actually had his time there listed on his acting resume. In reality, Bela was never a member of this prestigious theatrical group. As was often Bela's way, he exaggerated to boost his ego.

Bela did end up at the National Theater of Hungary, an acting institution with a prestigious past, but in no way comparable to the Academy of Theatrical Arts. As a member of the National Theater of Hungary, Bela gained the national exposure he had been seeking for so long a time. His initial taste of national acclaim came when he portrayed Shakespeare's Romeo, the tragic lover. A critic for *Mai Szinlap* wrote the following on this performance:

> Last night, Bela Lugosi, a new member of the troupe, demonstrated his artistic talent in the role of Romeo. The pleasant, handsome actor will certainly become one of the greats, judging by audience reaction to his performance.

Though the above review would swell any actor's head, especially one who was a relative novice to the arts, there were also those who did not care for Bela's acting ability. One such critic, Istvan Jeno, wrote about Bela in the drama *Az Ordog*, where one of the actor's most embarrassing moments occurred.

> As Bela Lugosi made his entrance, he couldn't even complete the first step before he tripped over a piece of carefully laid pipe. It propelled him onto the stage in a most undignified manner, causing him to overturn the easel and splatter his artistic smock with paint. The cast and the audience broke out into raucous fits of laughter, but the poor, bumbling actor jumped up nimbly, thoroughly embarrassed, and brushed himself off, ready to deliver his lines.

Regardless of what any drama critic may have written, Bela's performances were hungrily anticipated by the European theater-goers. Performance after performance, Bela received standing ovations; awards and honors were bestowed upon him and all of the European theatrical community were beginning to take notice of the name Bela Lugosi.

With his new-found fame, Bela Lugosi decided it was time to leave the Hungarian countryside and head for the big city. This meant more money and more recognition – not to mention more opportunities for his ego to continue to balloon. After his last performance in Szeged, acting in Arthur Schnitler's drama, *Anatol*, Hungary's most acclaimed and respected drama critic, Bela Kalmany, took the stage and paid tribute to the soon departing Lugosi.

> My friends, Szeged bids farewell to the intelligent actor with a handsome face and resonant voice we have come to know and appreciate during the past year. He has spoken to our hearts with a velvet voice, every bit a twentieth century actor. We have come to know and appreciate his ability to play so human a lover.
>
> Especially dear to me, of course, was his powerful performance as Romeo with an uncontrolled love and a heart full to bursting with tragedy as he views Juliet dead. When he utters the commonplace, he raises it to new heights and tragedy has never known such a craftsmen as Mr. Lugosi. Though his acting appears to be a natural gift, I have seen him develop his talents, through his daily struggles with characters. Alas, we must bid him farewell and even though we are saddened at the thought of his departure, I am sure that he will move the hearts of theater-goers, and especially those of the ladies, as he has moved ours.

Bela's entrance into the theatrical world in Budapest was met with great aplomb. Every time his name appeared atop a playbill, lines at the box office circled the long cobblestone blocks. Every time he walked out onto the stage, whether his initial entrance or for a new scene, the audience would stand as one and greet his appearance with thunderous applause. Although at this time he was by no means a master of his craft, he definitely was now the toast of the Hungarian and European dramatic community. With his career move to Budapest, Bela's life was finally going in the direction he had dreamed of in his hometown of Lugos. He had now proven those people who said he was a fool to runaway from home, quit school, and pursue a fantasy, wrong. He was an actor!

There he was, up on the Budapest stage with all of Europe in awe of his every move when World War I erupted.

On Sunday, June 28, 1914, an 18-year-old Serbian student, Gavrilo Princip, shot and killed Archduke Francis Ferdinand, heir to the throne of Austria-Hungary and nephew of Emperor Francis Joseph I. His wife, Duchess Sophie, also was slain. This double murder took place in Sarajevo, the ancient capital of Bosnia. Princip belonged to a secret terrorist organization whose members pledged to free Bosnia from Austrian rule and to unite it with Serbia. Princip saw his actions as a victory for liberty, but instead, they touched off World War I. This conflict lasted more than four years, involved over 30 nations, and claimed more than 20 million military and civilian lives. This cost billions of dollars, ravaged Europe, toppled kings and emperors, and sowed the seeds of World War II.

As troops from a multitude of nations invaded Europe for the bloodiest and most deadly war to date, Bela's career took a turn toward another stage – the battlefield. When Hungary entered the war, Bela was right there with his fellow countrymen. Upon his enlistment in the Hungarian military, Bela became a commissioned Second Lieutenant in the 43rd Infantry. Because of Hungary's geographic location, its military's main enemy was Russia, and the battles between the two were some of the worst of the war. Not only were the Hungarians battling for their homeland, they were also fighting for their survival as a people.

Because of his fame in his homeland, some may believe that Bela never saw "action," as was often the case with some American celebrities who served in the United States military during times of war. Nothing could be further from the truth. In his year-and-a-half with the 43rd Infantry, Bela fought in most of Hungary's bloodiest battles, and he did not come out of these battles unscathed. He nearly lost his life three times, and, according to some reports, carried a bullet in him from 1915 until his death in 1956.

During his time fighting with the 43rd Infantry, Bela received numerous awards for bravery, including the Hungarian equivalent to the United States military's Silver Star. He received this award for saving another soldier's life in the midst of a gun battle in the Carpathian Mountains (home territory of the real Count Dracula).

Bela once recounted one of his heroic acts. When his unit was protecting a forest from the Russians, a young officer ran out from cover and was struck in the chest by a bullet. Without regard for his own safety,

Bela ran out under machine-gun fire to give the soldier first aid. When he returned to the tree he had been hiding behind, Bela found it blown away.

Though Bela's account of the battle and his heroics are true, he did leave out one very important event. A mountainside, near where he was lying and crying, crumbled atop him because of the constant shelling around him. He was knocked unconscious by the rocks that cascaded down upon him and buried him alive under the rubble. When he was dug out, he was not breathing. Finally, after several attempts at resuscitation, he coughed up some blood and began breathing on his own.

After a year-and-a-half and three bloody battles, Bela was discharged from the Army, a changed man both physically (from his wounds, which included a bullet in the shoulder and one in the thigh) and politically. And then came his first marriage to Ilona Szmik, a young, beautiful woman from Budapest.

Not much is known about Bela's marriage to Ilona. Bela was quite the ladies' man and enjoyed female companionship of a sexual nature on a very regular basis, much more so than a usual marriage permits. Of course being the "sex symbol" that he was, these sexual urges posed no problem. His relationships with other women (both actresses and fans), while he was married to Ilona, were no secret (except apparently to Ilona). However, unlike the actors of today, he did not wear his sexual conquests on his sleeve like medals.

In 1935, when rumors surrounding the mystique of Bela Lugosi were as common in Hollywood as sex on the casting-room couch, Bela wrote a story about an extramarital affair he had while married to Ilona Szmik.

> She was an actress. She was not outstandingly beautiful. Her hair was pale brown. Her skin was deathly pale at times; at other times, it was blood red. Her mouth was thin and ravenous. Her teeth were tiny and pointed. She had been married many times; there had been many lovers. One never asked what had become of them. Men feared her – but went to her at command. Husbands left their wives because of her. I had a wife too. And two sons. Yes, I have two sons of whom I have never spoken. They are grown boys now. I have never seen them since I – I left. I have never, from that day to this, sent so much as a picture postcard home, nor have I had one. How should I? I burned all my bridges behind me when I left more than fifteen years ago. It was safer to have no communications of any earthly kind.

I wish that I could say that I did not care, that the thought of those two young men of mine did not matter to me, but I do care, it does matter. However, to get back ... At that time I was living a normal life as a young man of the town and I was said to be of outstanding appearance. I had a genial disposition and a happy outlook on life. Then I met her. The very first time I was introduced to her, I broke into deadly cold sweat. My heart and pulse raced and then seemed to stop dead! I lost control of my limbs and faltered in my speech. I was never happy in her presence. I felt always sick and dizzy and depleted. Yet, I could not remain away from her. She never bade me to come to her, not in words. There was never any of the conventional trappings of assignations. I simply went to her at odd hours of the day and night, impelled by an agency I neither saw nor heard. I lost weight. I hardly slept. I had seen other young men fade and wither before my eyes and had heard the village folks whisper in the dread cause. But when it came to me, I did not know it for what it was. It was my mother who forced me to flee the country and never to return to it again until that woman and every trace and memory of her vanished from the sight of men. This that I am telling you is the truth.

This story, written by Bela Lugosi about a supposed affair while he was married to Ilona, is pure fiction. This was written by Bela in 1935, four years after he made *Dracula*. Could it be that he was trying to tell film producers to come up with a featuring a female vampire? A film which would have him playing the romantic lead – a role he yearned for in Hollywood, yet never accomplished? (By the way, Bela had no children while he was living in Europe.)

With his release from the Army and his loss of bachelorhood, Bela once again headed back to the stages of the European theater in general, and the National Theater in particular. Upon his return to the National Theater, Bela realized how much things had changed in the theatrical community while World War I was being fought. The theater had once been an honor and privilege for the audience to attend; it was now nothing more than a respite from the anguishes of war; a human release from reality. Along with the change in the theater audience, there was also a new outlook toward stage actors. This so riled Bela that he felt he could not stand by without taking action. With these thoughts in mind, Bela started the first actors' equity in Europe (an actors' union). He did not know that certain political factions in Hungary were watching him and taking notes on his every movement at this time. A few years later, a Communist Party death contract was put out on him which caused him to flee his Motherland.

With the sudden downfall of the Hungarian stage production community, Bela focused his soon-to-be immortalized eyes on a new entertainment medium that was evolving in Hungary: motion pictures. When Bela entered the Hungarian film community, it was all of five years old. Unlike the film communities of other European countries or America, it was not meant to be the huge profit venture of foregoing art for the almighty dollar. It was meant to be a way to share the arts with a wider public and to bring classic literature to life. Also, unlike the other film communities, Hungarian filmmakers drafted only stage actors to perform in their films. The producers and directors wanted more than pretty faces; they wanted talent too.

Michael Curtiz was a Hungarian film director at the time of the birth of filmmaking in Hungary (and later went on to direct such American classics as *Casablanca*) He once said that Hungarian filmmaking was different from American filmmaking; Hungarian directors treated film as an art form, using real actors instead of just bodies. Curtiz believed Lugosi was destined to be a screen star.

Bela made his film debut for the Star Film Company in their production of *The Leipard*. Because he was skeptical of this new celluloid art form, he was not listed in the credits as Bela Lugosi, but by the singular name of Arisztid (which translates to "Aristocrat"). This was the only time Bela used an alias. When he found out that the film was critically praised and the art of making films was not a passing fancy, he reverted to Bela Lugosi.

Just how many films Bela made in Hungary is unknown, because quite a few of them were destroyed after communism moved into the land. Bela made his unadulterated hatred for communism public because those in power deemed it necessary to destroy as much of his work as they could find.

It was because of the political uprisings in Hungary and the artistic stifling of the dramatic community (both stage and film) that Bela formed the Free Organization of Theater Employees. Although Bela's aim was the "raising of the moral, economic, and cultural level of the actor's society," not all involved with the entertainment society were pleased with this movement. At one point, the Budapest Theater Society started a countermovement and demanded Bela's banishment from the stage and screen. The Budapest Theater Society's demands fell on deaf ears, not because they were wrong, but because the name Bela Lugosi created profits from anything he was associated with.

When Hungary found itself in yet another political uprising, the new politically active Bela Lugosi became a voice people wanted to hear. When the surrounding government began to topple, Bela not only backed Count Michael Karolyi, a want-to-be leader; but, he also put his clout behind him and wrote the following copy for a Budapest newspaper. He had hoped to rally his fellow actors to join his quest to put Karolyi in office:

> After putting aside the glamorous trappings of his trade at the end of each performance, an actor had, with few exceptions, to face worry and poverty. He was obliged either to bend himself to stultifying odd jobs to keep body and soul together (while of course being unavailable for work in his true profession) or he had to sponge off his friends, go into debt, or prostitute his art. And he endured it; endured the poverty, the humiliation, the exploitation, just so that he could continue to be an actor, to get parts, for without them he could not live. Actors were exploited no less by the private capitalist managers than they were by the state. The former ruling class kept the actors' community in ignorance by means of various lies, corrupted it morally and materially, and finally scorned and despised it, for what resulted from its own vices. Martyrdom was the price of enthusiasm for acting.

Bela's ploy of getting his fellow performers behind Michael Karolyi did work. Karolyi replaced the head of the Hungarian government, even though it was for a very short time. What Bela's novice political mind failed to understand was that there was a "dark" political power surrounding Hungary which had the backing of large amounts of money and included the top propaganda purveyors. Miklos Horthy and his Romanian forces headed this rising political power. Horthy would let no one stand in the way of what he wanted, namely the country of Hungary.

When Miklos Horthy assumed political power in Hungary, one of his first proclamations called for the arrest, imprisonment, and execution of those who were sympathizers of the government he fought to overthrow. Among the names on Horthy's "hit list" were Paul Lukas, Alexander Korda, Michael Curtiz, and, of course, Bela Lugosi. Because he was a proud man, Bela did not flee his Motherland without one last shot at Miklos Horthy and those in the arts that he felt were contemptible. Bela's last "shot" was an article he wrote, titled "Love the Actor," which was reluctantly published by Szineszek Lapsa on May 15, 1919. Bela added to this article large portions from his article backing Michael Karolyi, an article that was so popular and galvanizing that it helped put Karolyi in power.

Love the actor, for he gives you his heart! It has been said more than once by our comrades – some of them, moreover, in the highest ranks of our leadership – that actors are not proletarian. Let us look at that statement. Since we assume no malice was intended, we must impute this erroneous opinion to total ignorance. What is the truth? It is that 95 percent of the actors' community has been more proletarian than the most exploited laborer. After putting aside the glamorous trappings of his trade at the end of each performance, an actor had, with few exceptions, to face worry and poverty. He was obliged either to bend himself to stultifying odd jobs to keep body and soul together or he had to sponge off his friends, get into debt, or prostitute his art. And he endured it, endured the poverty, the humiliation, the exploitation, just so that he could not live. Actors were exploited no less by the private capitalist managers that they were by the state. The current rulers have kept the community of actors in ignorance by means of various lies, corrupted it morally and materially. The actor, subsisting on starvation wages and demoralized, is often driven, albeit, reluctantly, to place himself at the disposal of the current rulers!

The reason that Bela wrote from an actor's point of view is quite simple: the public does not like their heroes driven down. And, since Bela and his fellow actors were considered heroes within their country, he knew writing in such a way would gain the notice of the public.

By the time his feelings were printed for all to read, Bela Lugosi and his wife had fled Hungary and were headed for Austria, where they settled in Vienna.

Whereas the artistic life for Bela Lugosi had been good in Hungary, it was so in Vienna. Although his reputation of being a fine stage and screen actor did indeed follow him to Austria, so did his politics. Those who oversaw the Austrian stage community (a screen community was virtually nonexistent in Austria in 1919) basically blacklisted him because of Bela's political reputation. Finding work in the entertainment industry became nearly impossible for Bela. As his professional ego was being beaten and his money was rapidly disappearing, he was hit with another personal blow. Ilona left him and filed for divorce. Once Ilona returned to Hungary and the open arms of her parents, Bela knew there was no hope for a reconciliation. If he set foot in Hungary, he would be killed!

Concerning the breakup of his marriage, Bela once stated, "In all his life a man finds only one mate. Other women may bring happiness close to him, but there is just one mate. The girl was mine. Possibly she was too young and fragile and lacked the necessary stalwart character to fight her way through." In saying, "fight her way through," Bela was referring to his problems with the Hungarian government and his fleeing Hungary to save his own life.

Though Bela was upset at being left by Ilona, he didn't go through a mourning period. Even before Ilona was on Hungarian soil, Bela was cavorting openly with the most beautiful women Vienna had to offer. And, being the romanticist that he was, he loved to brag about his conquests.

On one occasion in the late 1930's, Bela described an encounter that was right out of the film *Dracula*. Like the vampire Count, he seduced his female victims. The story is at least partially true, even though Bela often added fictional accounts to his real-life exploits.

The man who was once the toast of the European stage was now a beaten individual who, according to some reports, contemplated suicide. His professional world was crumbling into a heap around him. This is when Bela made a major decision regarding his artistic life. The choice to be weighed was whether he should give his full concentration to the stage or to the screen. Coming to the realization that his talents would reach more people via the screen, he once again packed his bags and headed to Berlin. There, filmmaking was treated as a "true" art form and, more important, American directors and producers were searching for new talent.

Shortly after arriving in Berlin, Bela found work within the cinematic community, although not as the headline star he had been in Hungary. In his first film, *Sklaven Femdes Willens* (*Slave of a Foreign Will*), he portrayed a hypnotist who seduced young women. Although his role was not considered to be in the horror genre, Bela's presence in the role (especially his physical movements) created an aura of the occult.

While working in the German cinema, Bela ran across a few people who would touch his life when he reached America. One was the German film director, F.W. Murnau, who, a few years after directing Bela in *Der Januskopf* (an unauthorized version of Robert Louis Stevenson's *Dr. Jekyll and Mr. Hyde*), made *Nosferatu The Vampire*. It was the first cinematic treatment of Bram Stoker's *Dracula* (a film which was banned in many countries due to lawsuits from Mrs. Stoker and its unadulterated use of horror in a visual form). Another one was the legendary cinematographer, Karl Freund, who was solely responsible for the way Bela appeared in the film *Dracula*. This included making his eyes the most famous in the history of the American cinema (caused by an error in lighting).

Although his professional life was beginning to flourish once again, his personal life was still void of a woman with whom to share his life. In 1921, for reasons only Bela himself knew, he married for a second time. Wife number two was a beautiful blond Austrian who came from a wealthy family. Her name was Ilona Montaugh de Nagybanyhegyes and though Bela claimed he married because of true love, others believed it was simply because he needed to fill the void in his life. Whatever his reasons may have been, Bela was once again smiling, both mentally and physically.

While performing on the German screen, Bela's roles varied. He was often cast in the role of the bad guy because of his deliberate mannerisms and menacing good looks. He didn't mind; it gave him more of a chance to improvise his roles. This was a side of Bela Lugosi that American audiences never got a chance to see because Hollywood studio moguls, for the most part, prohibited actors from showing that they could be more than studio robots.

The American market noticed the German cinema; Bela's talents were watched from across the Atlantic. The legendary studio mogul, Samuel Goldwyn, after viewing Bela on screen for the first time is said to have screamed, "I've found the new Valentino!"

When he heard he was being talked about by American filmmakers, Bela Lugosi made the most important decision he would ever make. He decided to go to the land of opportunity: America.

CHAPTER TWO

AMERICA, THE BEAUTIFUL

I feel I am an awfully lucky person to be an American and I think that every naturalized American and every person born in this land should kneel on his knees every morning and utter a prayer for being an American.
                    Bela Lugosi on becoming an American citizen.

When Bela Lugosi left Germany for the United States of America, the German film community was going full-force, despite the economic ruin the country was going through. Leaving Germany then meant giving up a certain superstar status, a quest that, up until that time, had been his ultimate career goal.

Because Bela had lost most of his money running from the political vengeance that seemed to be chasing him, to get to America, he had to toil for a living. After a couple of weeks of searching for a way to get to the "land of the free," Bela stumbled upon a job which would not only pay him enough money for his journey, but would actually take him on the journey. He gave up his life as a thespian, albeit for only a short time, to become a seaman on the Italian freighter christened the *Count Stefan Tisza*. Everything was going as Bela planned, although he did find that being a seaman was physically a lot more work than treading the boards at a theater. Just as he was getting his "sea feet," things started to change for the worst.

Somehow some of the freighter's crew found out about Bela's political preferences (the crew was mainly communist and Bela was very anticommunist). In a matter of hours, the word spread throughout the freighter and by nightfall his life was in peril. While Bela slept below deck on his bed of wooden crates cushioned with tarpaulin, the other seamen were devising ways to put an end to their recently hired shipmate. Their ultimate goal, a burial at sea!

The crew's original plan, if rumors are to be believed, was to have Bela beaten with a mast support and thrown over the side of the ship. The concocted story to cover up the murder was that Bela, being a naive and novice seaman, while working erratically was struck on the head with the mast support and was knocked overboard. When a few of the crew complained that this was not a plausible plan because its was so remotely believable, the plan was scratched.

The second plan, which was carried out, was indeed rather simple. They would severely beat Bela and toss him overboard to be the *cuisine du jour* for the sharks in the infested waters of the Atlantic Ocean. According to reports, it was late at night; and while Bela slept, the devious crew members who had devised the malicious plan drank heavily and talked Communist politics. As the liquor began to flow as turbulently as the sea they were crossing, the crew became more boisterous about their feelings about their Hungarian shipmate and his political leanings. About two hours later, guided by the alcohol they had consumed, they ventured to the below deck lodgings where Bela was sleeping. On the way to Bela's cabin, the drunk seamen picked up various tools of destruction (e.g. wood clubs, construction tools, etc.).

As the Italian seamen were making their way to Bela's cabin, their boisterous activities woke Bela out of his deep sleep. The moment his feet hit the floor, the door flew open. Much to Bela's surprise, he was confronted by those he once had believed to be friends. Before Bela could open his mouth to inquire about the rude intrusion, one of the seamen leapt at him, followed by the others.

What these Italian seamen did not know was that Bela knew how to take care of himself physically. He fought the seamen the best he could; the ruckus woke the ship's captain, who proceeded to follow the riotous noises. As soon as the captain entered Bela's cabin and saw what was going on, he ordered his men out of the cabin and commanded the ships medic to look Bela over. Bela sustained no serious injuries, only a few cuts and lacerations. Amazingly enough, Bela's face was unscathed with the exception of split and swollen lips. When the ship's medic concluded his examination of Bela, all of the seamen were ordered to their quarters until an investigation into the activities could be conducted and concluded by the ship's captain.

When the captain finished his investigation into the attack on Bela, he found himself in a quandary. He knew the attack was wrong and that his crew was totally at fault. However, this was his crew and his fellow countrymen that he had to work with on a daily basis. Along these same lines, the captain knew he had to keep Bela safe. If he went into an American port with a corpse to unload, American authorities would conduct their own investigation. There was only one move the captain could make: he placed Bela under protective custody (arrest) as a stowaway. Then he destroyed all physical records of Bela working as an employee on the *Count Stefan Tisza*. For the remainder of the ship's voyage, according to ship records, Bela was a prisoner in his own cabin for a little more than two weeks. He was allowed to leave only with the ship's captain as his personal escort.

Because the *Count Stefan Tisza* was carrying cargo, its first stop in the United States was New Orleans. As soon as the ship docked, the captain notified the proper authorities of his stowaway. When Bela was brought on deck, his once viral frame looked gaunt, his color was a sickly pale, and the fire which once roared in his eyes had been reduced to dying embers of hopelessness. As the authorities were leading Bela away, he gave a merciful look to the captain of the *Count Stefan Tisza*, followed by a weak salute. In retrospect, it is assumed that this salute was Bela's way of thanking the captain for saving his life.

Because of the political atmosphere of the world at this time, Bela was not placed under arrest upon disembarking from the ship. He was taken to the local police station and from there he was forwarded to what can only be described as a "safe-house." According to the plan of the authorities, he was to stay in the safe-house until a hearing could be arranged for possible deportation. The hearing never took place.

What the seafaring Bela Lugosi did not know was that his sailing to the United States was highly anticipated by the Hungarian Literary Society. This group of Hungarian artists had immigrated to New York City to escape political prosecution in their Motherland. They knew how much "red tape" it took to stay in America and be accepted by the immigration authorities. They took it upon themselves to draw up a Declaration for

Immigration to the United States in Bela's name. This Declaration read as follows:

> We who know of the activities of Bela Lugosi during the period of the Councits' Republic due to our association and membership in organization which were under his direct administration, state with pleasure and pride for those who are hostile or partial to rumors based on little information that during the Councits' Republic, Bela Lugosi was the secretary of the Actors' Trade Union. He was elected to the position by the majority vote of his peers, fellow actors. The Actors' Trade Union was founded in order to protect the rights of its members and WAS NOT involved in politics. The activities of the Trade Union were directed by officers elected by all the actors. Bela Lugosi was the secretary and, as such, only an executor of the decisions made by the leadership. We solemnly declare that Bela Lugosi did nothing except sacrifice his health, rising career, and family life to serve faithfully the interests of the actors for which recognition and gratitude should be due him. Under no circumstances did any of his actors shame or cause injury to the Hungarian people or nation.

This declaration was in the hands of the immigration authorities when Bela walked off the *Count Stefan Tisza and* because of this, a deportation hearing was never held. The immigration authorites turned Bela over to the First Hungarian Literary Society's authorities. After this "human transfer," Bela headed directly for New York City where the society was headquartered.

During his life in Europe, Bela had always heard that New York City was a mecca for actors. So, when he found out this city was going to be his first American home, he became ecstatic. He was an actor of international acclaim and now he was in New York City! There was one problem though; Bela could not speak a single word of English.

Stagnation was never a word associated with the life and career of Bela Lugosi and this point is vividly illustrated in regard to Bela's move to New York City. Even though he was new to America and could not speak the language, this did not stop him from continuing his artistic craft. Within months after his arrival in New York City, Bela formed a Hungarian Repertory Company in which he starred, produced, and directed all

Figure 2 – Throughout Dracula, *Karl Freund used shadows to perfection to create a new art form in cinematography. It was still the hynotic eyes of Bela which caught the attention of filmgoers. (Copyright © 1931 by Universal Studios, Inc. Courtesy of MCA Publishing Rights, a Division of MCA Inc. All Rights Reserved)*

productions. And, he hired Hungarian playwrights to pen the productions the company presented.

Although Bela's first works on the American stage were totally Hungarian and observed by very few theater-goers, he did catch the eyes of those who mattered. The industry moguls of both the stage and the cinema noticed. Their curiosity toward Bela might have been because of a theatrical advertisement which originally ran in a Berlin newspaper that made its rounds in the American theatrical and cinema community shortly after Bela arrived on the shores of America. The ad read as follows:

> Bela Lugosi is a famous Hungarian artist. Among his leading roles were Karl Mohr, William Tell, Romeo, Manfred, Armandi, Cyrano de Bergerac, and others. Since 1912, he has been a member of the National Theater of Hungary where he played heroic, romantic leads and has become a favorite with audiences due to favorable recognition by the press. As a film actor, he experienced as much success in Budapest as he does in Berlin.

This ad contained everything American theatrical and cinematic moguls looked for, from press recognition by the harsh European theater critics to the adulation of the German cinematic community which was the envy of the world at this time. The person who wrote this ad for the Berlin newspaper was indeed quite aware of Bela's artistic achievements, though obviously somewhat prejudiced. The writer was Bela Lugosi.

The question is: "Where did Bela get the money to produce the plays by his Hungarian Repertory Company?"

The answer to this question is threefold. First, all members of the company paid dues, whatever they could afford with no mandatory qualifications. Second, the Hungarian community in and around New York contributed to the repertory coffers. And third, Bela's wife, Ilona Montaugh de Nagybanyhegyes, joined him in America shortly after his arrival and brought with her the money that they had saved in Europe (contrary to rumor, Bela and his second wife, Nagybanyhegyes, were not married in New York City).

After numerous productions with the repertory company, Bela was wondering why no American film or stage roles were offered to him. He did not consider that all of the work he was doing was in his native language and that very few people outside of the Hungarian community saw his talents.

28

Late 1921, while Bela was starring in his own production of *The Tragedy of Man* at New York City's Lexington Theater, a man who did not understand a single word of the Hungarian witnessed what he later described as "the grace and stage elegance of a natural born actor." This man, Henry Barron, was an off-Broadway impressiaro. As Henry Barron watched Bela tread the hardwood stage of the Lexington Theater, he came to the conclusion that he wanted Bela Lugosi for the lead in a new production. It was an American version of the French play *The Red Poppy*. Barron was unaware that Bela could not speak English.

After Bela's performance of *The Tragedy of Man*, Henry Barron went backstage to meet the actor who had piqued his creative mind. It was at this point that Barron realized that Bela's knowledge of the English language amounted to nothing.

In talking with Bela through an interpreter, Barron was very impressed with Bela's theatrical determination. Bela was so enthralled by the chance to appear in a major production that he made the following statement to Barron (through an interpreter): "Give me a chance. Give me a tutor, take his salary out of my future earnings, and by the time you are ready to start rehearsals, I will know my part."

Taking Bela at his word, Henry Barron had a standard contract drawn up with one stipulation; Bela must learn English well enough to play the part of Fernando, an Apache Indian.

In an effort to learn the language quickly (Bela had only twelve weeks until the start of rehearsals for *The Red Poppy*), Bela took the unconventional approach to learning only his lines phonetically. With the assistance of the repertory members who could speak English, Bela learned his role by mimicking those who were reading the lines to him in English. At the end of the 12 weeks, the only English Bela Lugosi could speak were his lines in *The Red Poppy*.

On December 20, 1922, Bela Lugosi made his debut in an American production of *The Red Poppy* with an English speaking role at the Greenwich Village Theater and was a critical smash. In John Corbin's review of this production for *The New York Times* on December 21, 1922, Bela Lugosi is described as "romantically handsome" and "an actor of fine achievement and possibly greater promise."

The late Estelle Winwood, star of *The Red Poppy*, remembered Bela's legitimate American stage debut:

He was so nervous, we were all wondering if he'd be able to

perform, but once he walked onto the stage and the lights hit him, he was truly magical. Though he was new to the American stage, it was obvious to all who knew about the theater that he was classically trained. His movements were so poetic, though his strength was absolutely animalistic – as was his sexual magnetism.

Winwood spoke from experience about Bela's strength and sexual magnetism. She had been on the receiving end of both. In her role of Princess Saratoff, Winwood had numerous romantic scenes with Bela. And in one, which had the two in a steamy lovemaking scene, it is reported that Bela cracked several of her ribs (this was an off-Broadway production where simulated sex was not uncommon, a reversal of the "bluenose" production under the neon along the Great White Way).

Once the word of Bela's performance hit the streets, interest in *The Red Poppy* intensified and crowds at the box office were gathering in droves (and of course the inclusion of sex in the production didn't hurt). After six weeks of performances at the Greenwich Theater, Henry Barron took the production to Broadway. Because of the explicit sex scenes, this attempt proved futile and the play closed. If rumors are to be believed, though, the sex between Winwood and Bela was more than just "acting."

While the run of *The Red Poppy* was in progress, most of Bela's free time was taken up with learning English, or the American version of it. As his reviews were being read to him by members of his repertory company, he came to realize that stardom could be his if he applied himself, most importantly, to learning the language.

With the play going on at night, his classes in the language during most days and his sexual dalliances with Winwood somewhere in between, Bela's wife, Ilona, was becoming more and more frustrated with their marriage. In early 1923, she decided that Bela should make a choice. Bela did not choose his marriage to Ilona.

When it was obvious that Bela's second marriage was headed for divorce court, Ilona, well aware of Bela's extramarital escapades, made the following statement (which surprised no one): "Bela was a fiery lover offstage as well as on. As a lover, he was a brilliant success, but as a husband, well, he was simply a fiasco!"

When news of Ilona's statement reached the trade papers, Bela felt he had to counter and relay his thoughts on marriage. He said, in marriage, it is the woman's responsibility to get along with the man. He also made it known that he thought a woman's place was in the home, taking care of her husband and children.

Such a statement today would have leaders of the woman's movement calling for Bela's head. However, the time and arena where Bela was raised was different. He was a man from the "old country" of Europe and, regarding the sacrament of marriage, he did believe what he said to be true. As Bela became somewhat more Americanized in his way of thinking, his thoughts on holy matrimony did soften, though not much.

When the marriage of Bela Lugosi and Ilona was legally dissolved, Ilona gave the press her final say on the matter. She said that, even though they had a romantic relationship, there was too much artistic temperament on both sides. Bela's jealousy caused her to give up acting to try to make a go of their marriage.

There don't seem to be any cast rosters in either Europe or America with Ilona's name listed as a player. As the facts have proven through the years, Ilona could stretch the truth almost as well as Bela Lugosi himself.

During the time when Bela and Ilona were going through their verbal sparring matches and contemplating divorce, a new avenue of the American entertainment industry was opening up to him. Knocking on Bela's professional door was opportunity in the cinema.

After seeing Bela's performance in *The Red Poppy*, Edward Small, an executive at Fox Pictures, took notice of the way Bela's stage presence captured the entire audience. Small believed that if Bela could do this on the stage, he could only magnify it on film.

When he returned to the offices of Fox Pictures in Hollywood, Edward Small told everyone who would listen of his discovery in New York City. After a production meeting for the soon-to-be-shot motion picture, *The Silent Command*, the films producer and director agreed to Small's request for Bela to portray Hisston, the villainous spy. Neither Small nor Fox Pictures was concerned about Bela's lack of English language skills because the film was a silent picture.

To say that Bela was a "hit" in *The Silent Command* would be a gross understatement. Although the film was panned by the critics, they did notice the acting ability of Bela Lugosi. Each of the critics paid special attention to one point: the effectiveness of Bela's ability to portray horror and evil in such a realistic way. One critic summed up Bela's portrayal of the evil Hisston saying, "Hisston, say it with snake-like sibilance, is the villain, and never was there a more snaky international trickster."

As with quite a few films during this era in Hollywood, *The Silent Command* was a propaganda vehicle. The message sent to the American film-goer was quite simple and, in retrospect, quite obvious; the American military needed a large Navy (the film centers on the Navy and spies trying to infiltrate it). A few years after making *The Silent Command*, Bela commented about his first American film as a piece of propaganda.

> I used to smile at the thought that, for this preachment, a Hungarian star had been chosen as the chief propagandist, since Hungary has no Navy nor needs any.

Although he obviously did not realize it at the time, his powerful performance in *The Silent Command* began the process of typecasting Bela Lugosi.

Sometime after Bela realized this, he explained his thoughts in an interview:

> In spite of the predominance of romantic roles in my reper-toire, when I came to America I found that because of my language and the pantomime, with which most Europeans ac-company their speech, that I was cataloged as what you call "a heavy." And, at once I became identified with that class of performance. Particularly was this true in pictures where, strangely enough, no accent could be registered, since pictures in those days were silent. If my accent betrayed my foreign birth it also stamped me, in the imagination of the producers, as "an enemy." Therefore, I must be a heavy.

After his initial venture in Hollywood for the making of *The Silent Command* (which also took Bela to Panama to film on location), Bela returned to New York City. When he came back to New York, Bela found more stage roles and began to improve his English by using very special tutors: the women with whom he had liaisons. In exchange for the service of these tutors, Bela allowed them to fulfill their fantasy of being with an actor. Under these conditions, Bela rapidly learned the language, which would garner him an income for the rest of his life.

Between the various stage productions, Bela would take whatever parts were offered him by independent film producers. One such role was in the 1925 film, *The Midnight Girl*. In this rather forgettable silent film,

Bela played a millionaire patron of the opera who had a weakness for beautiful women, perhaps evidence that life imitates art. Bela's leading lady in *The Midnight Girl* was the beautiful Lila Lee and in the film Bela vied for her affection against his stepson. It was a stereotypical Bela Lugosi role and, even though he lost out on her attentions in the film, he won them when Lila Lee helped him in private with his language studies.

Although, Bela jumped from stage productions to film, he preferred the art of the cinema. In an interview a couple of years later, after the release of *Dracula*, when his career was almost solely cinematic, Bela commented:

> It is the greatest medium of expression an actor knows. While the stage is near and will always be dear to me, I cannot truthfully say I would rather be back on the stage. While it is true that a screen actor has no audience before him other than his fellow workers, he is nevertheless compensated in the knowledge that millions will see his performance at one time, where only hundreds could see it on the stage.

Between small film roles, Bela did have the chance to sink his teeth into (pun intended) his first horror production – a 1924 stage adaptation of *The Werewolf* (a reworking of a German play. It did not at all resemble the Lon Chaney Jr. classic horror film, *The Wolf Man*). Leslie Howard, an up-and-coming young actor, was also featured in this film. Because this American adaptation was so overtly sexual , the critics slammed it with such force that it vibrated the shutters on the buildings of Broadway following its closing.

In the years between 1924 and 1927, Bela finally left the small and often rancid-smelling confines of the off-Broadway theaters and appeared under the glowing neon lights of the "legitimate" theaters of Broadway. While holding audiences and critics were in awe of his mysterious talents in plays, such as *Arabesque* and *The Devil in the Cheese*, something big was unfolding across the Atlantic Ocean in the theater district of London. A play was being readied for a major stage production starring Raymond Huntley: *Dracula*.

The London stage version of *Dracula* was quite different from the version that would soon appear in America. The play in London was produced more for shock value than Victorian elegance and grace. For instance, Raymond Huntley, the British Count Dracula wore freakish makeup to appeal to British audiences. This freakishness was not at all like the romantic persona portrayed by Bela Lugosi. Huntley also donned a partial mask, much like the Phantom in *The Phantom of the Opera,* the Andrew Lloyd Webber musical extravaganza which recently set Broadway box office records.

When the London stage adaptation of *Dracula* wowed the usually stoic British critics, a few American stage producers began to take notice. It turned quite serious when these producers realized that the London version of *Dracula* was breaking all box office records. Money always piques a producer's interest and big audiences always equal big dollars.

The American producer Horace Liveright took London's *Dracula* sensation by the reins and ran with it. After going through all the hassles of buying the American rights to *Dracula* (including a legal fight or two with the lawyers of Mrs. Bram Stoker), the papers were finally signed and the hoopla surrounding this major work began.

The one thing Horace Liveright wanted to change from the London version of *Dracula* was the genuine-horror focus of the play. He knew this approach would not appeal to the American theater critics, nor the usual audiences of the grand theatrical houses. Liveright hired producer John Balderston, a writer respected in both the literary and theatrical communities, to make the artistic changes Liveright wanted. While Balderston was rewriting the London version of the play, Liveright asked some of his stage-director friends to keep an eye out for an actor to play the title role. It was Jean D. Williams who found Bela Lugosi.

In an interview with the Hungarian newspaper, *Szinhaz es Mori Ojsag,* Bela reflected on his meeting with Jean D. Williams:

> Two years ago, I was playing the lead role in *Open House* on Broadway. Jean D. Williams, the famous director of *Rain,* saw me in that production and he told me that I appealed to him in the role so much that he finally asked me to see him about another role. He had already prepared a stage adaptation of *Dracula,* but it was not like the one currently being shown in New York. He believed that I was the only actor in America who was suitable for the part and wanted me to audition.

This describes Bela's initial meeting with Jean D. Williams; Bela was obviously confused about two items. First, Williams had nothing to do with the American adaptation of the play and, second, there was no other version of *Dracula* being performed in New York (or anywhere else in North America). Also, Bela did not know Horace Liveright was in negotiations to bring Raymond Huntley, to play the title role in the American version of *Dracula*. Negotiations eventually broke down when Huntley's monetary requests did not match what Liveright was willing to offer.

In July 1927, Bela Lugosi finally had his opportunity to audition for the role of Count Dracula. Bela was once said, "There was no male vampire type in existence. Someone suggested an actor of the Continental School who could play any type, and mentioned me. It was a complete change from the usual romantic characters I was playing, but it was a success."

Obviously, Bela did get the role. But, when he was first offered the role of Count Dracula, he read the entire script and he did not like it. As the star of the production, he thought he would speak a majority of the lines, which was not the case at all. While his actor's ego was deflating, Bela informed Horace Liveright of his discontent. Liveright tried to convince Bela that although his lines were minimal, they were lines that the audience would remember and lines that they would keep them on the edge of their seats. Bela still balked at the role. Liveright walked out of the audition hall and gave Bela the following parting words: "Okay. Fine. Don't take the role. I won't lose any sleep over it and I sure won't lose any money, something you won't be able to say!"

It was the word money that caught Bela's attention; he then signed on for the play. It is interesting to note that although Bela's command of the English language was still lacking, this was one of the reasons why he got the part. Horace Liveright liked the authenticity of Bela's accent and thought it would add significantly to the role.

On September 25, 1927, in New Haven, Connecticut, the American stage adaptation of *Dracula* opened with Bela starring in his first "big budget" American stage production. The New Haven opening was to work out all the production glitches before the play moved to Broadway. As it turned out, the only glitches were Bela's. According to Liveright, his movements were robotic. But, by the time the play was ready for New York City and the awaiting media blitz, Bela had his lines down to perfection, including his pronunciations. And, his stage movements were pure grace (just as they are in the film version).

On October 5, 1927, *Dracula* made its Broadway debut at the Fulton Theater. From the moment that the theater lights dimmed, the audience was spellbound and the critics were ecstatic. That is, with the exception of

Brook Atkinson of *The New York Times*. In Atkinson's review on October 6, 1927, he wrote that Bela was, "like the performance, a little too deliberate and confident."

On the other end of the criticism spectrum, another reviewer wrote that there hadn't been any performance "more blood curdling since *The Bat*," and that Bela's build and accent made him a "really sinister" Count.

It was not just this one theater enthusiast who was unnerved by the production of *Dracula*. Within the first week, eight members of the audience had to be treated for shock. After this particular audience reaction to the production, Horace Liveright, inserted the following disclaimer in a banner-headline layout in all ads for the play:

A NURSE WILL BE IN ATTENDANCE
AT ALL PERFORMANCES.

After 33 weeks and 241 performances at the Fulton Theater -- all before standing room only audiences -- the stage version of *Dracula* closed and went on the road for a national tour. By the time *Dracula* left New York, it had earned $350,857.50 in receipts (and this was in 1927 and 1928, when a dollar was worth more). Also, by this time, Bela Lugosi's talents had been noticed by everyone in both the theatrical and cinematic communities. Bela Lugosi was now an entertainment force to be reckoned with.

In 1936, shortly before he was to don the black cape of Count Dracula for the film version, Bela talked about the stage role which garnered him such fame.

> After I had been in the play for a month, I began to take stock of myself, and I realized that for my own well being I should make some attempt to conserve my mental and physical strength – to throw myself with less fervor into the depiction of the role. By that time I knew every inflection, every movement, every expression required of the character and I decided that if I could go through the play somewhat mechanically – somewhat more placidly within myself – there would be no lessening of the effect on my own nervous system.
>
> But I could not do it. The role seemed to demand that I keep myself worked up to a fever pitch, and so I sat in my dressing room and took on, as nearly as possible, the actual attributes of

incident centered on Bela Lugosi himself and his eyes. According to Dorothy Peterson (Lucy Harker), Bernard Jukes (Renfield), and Edward Van Sloan (Dr. Van Helsing), the following occurred on more than one occasion. Each time they witnessed it, the fear in their voices and the frightened look on their faces were indeed very real.

According to all three of Bela's co-stars, there were times on stage when the script called for Bela, as Dracula, to look into their eyes. His own eyes began to change color; the whites of his eyes turning a blood red and, as they got redder and redder, all three actors claimed they could feel a burning sensation in their bodies. During one of these instances when Dorothy Peterson was the victim, the fear in her became so intense that she felt she was going to faint. It is unlikely that this was a publicity gimmick, because all three actors talked about it long after both the play and the film were out of public circulation.

What caused Bela's eyes to turn blood red is unknown (if in fact they really did), but according to Edward Van Sloan (Dr. Van Helsing in both the play and the film):

> Bela was the most intense actor I've ever shared a scene with. Perhaps the reason the whites of his eyes sometimes turned blood red may be because his hypnotic stare, both in character and out, was so intense he broke blood vessels in his eyes. Perhaps – but perhaps not.

As Bela's star status began to rise, so did his infamous womanizing. Outside his dressing room door at the Fulton Theater in New York City, there were always "groupies" waiting to fall under the elegant actor's sexual spell. According to his fellow cast members, Bela never went home alone and he never ventured out with the same woman twice. This was not the case when the play moved west to California.

On the opening night of *Dracula* at the Biltmore in Los Angeles, Clara Bow, Hollywood's famous "it" girl sat in the front row. From the moment Bela swept onto the stage, Clara Bow was smitten. Every move that Bela made was eagerly watched by Bow's famous batting eyes. As the opening night performance came to its conclusion, Bow ran backstage to meet the man under whose spell she had fallen.

Clara Bow was known in Hollywood for her sexual prowess. It did not matter whether it was a man or woman, as long as her insatiable thirst was appeased. Bow was never one to openly exploit those who were involved with her. So, it wasn't until Daisy DeVoe, Bow's personal assistant, was accused of extortion that all of her secrets came out. According to DeVoe, so liberal was Clara Bow with her sexual favors that, on many an evening, Bow had men waiting outside her bedroom for their chance to be with her.

The Clara Bow/Bela Lugosi escapades were the talk of Hollywood while *Dracula* played at the Biltmore. Every night, after each performance, Bela and Clara would hit the town's hot spots and, after a few drinks and a tango or two, the couple would head back to Bow's abode to continue the night's entertainment.

The frantic sexual encounters between Bela and Bow lasted only a few short weeks. The reason for this was Bela's Old World way of looking at male/female relationships. As the couple began spending more and more time together, Bela was making demands on Bow. Because she was such an independent woman, she found his ways to be completely stifling. Bow, although enamored of Bela, could not be monogamous, as Bela demanded. When their affair ended, it was indeed a parting of the ways. Bela went to San Francisco with the play; and Bow, without missing a beat, went into the arms of yet another Hollywood hunk!

When *Dracula* opened at the Columbia Theater in San Francisco, the farthest thing from Bela's mind was a third marriage. At a party after the opening night, Bela was the focus of everyone's attention. His performance cast a spell over the entire audience. And, like other cities where he had performed, women were spellbound. One of the women at this party was Beatrice Weeks, an uppity widow of one of the city's most influential men (not to mention part owner of the city's landmark hotel, the Mark Hopkins). What exactly happened at this party between Bela and Beartice Weeks is unknown. But, a few days later they were married in a public ceremony attended by Bela's fellow cast members and some of Beatrice's close friends.

The most interesting item about this newlywed's relationship was that Beatrice Weeks was the exact opposite of what Bela felt a woman should be. Beatrice was a "woman's libber" before the term was ever conceived. She smoked and could drink Bela under the table. She was not a doting wife who felt her man should be treated like a king. And, she was not the type of woman who would take orders. She demanded that she be an equal in every sense of the word.

Proof that opposites who attract, do not necessarily make a marriage that lasts; Bela Lugosi and Beatrice Weeks lasted an amazing four days as husband-and-wife. According to Weeks, on the fourth morning of their marriage, they had their final conversation. She had a rather large hangover and Bela looked at her with disgust. He said he had told her to give up gin or get out of his house. He said he wouldn't stand for this every morning of his life

Beatrice wondered how Bela could change so much in just four days. She told him that he had to take her for what she was, not what he wanted her to be. She said she couldn't give up her past or her identity, not even for him.

With his now famous snarl in his voice, he told her to pack her bags and get out! She had to remind him that he was living in her penthouse and if anyone was going to leave, it would be him. Taking a deep breath, he headed for the door and his final words were to file for divorce and place the blame on him for incompatibility. He said there wouldn't be any problems; he didn't want her money.

Although Bela's San Francisco stay may have been carnage on a personal level, on an artistic level, he was the toast of the town. The morning after his San Francisco *Dracula* debut, *The San Francisco Chronicle*, wrote that the performance was a grisly, ghastly, glorious feast of fiendish inequities – a revel of horrendous happenings . . ." They further stated that Bela's portrayal of Dracula had "considerable power."

By the time the stage production of *Dracula* ended its West Coast engagement (San Francisco, Oakland, and Los Angeles), it had grossed $108,080.00. *Dracula* became the largest box office hit in theatrical history. As the play made plans to head back to New York City, Bela decided to stay in Hollywood. He had become more involved with the cinema (making films during off hours while performing in *Dracula* on stage). The person chosen to replace Bela's leading role was the producer's first choice for the part – Raymond Huntley.

When Bela Lugosi hung up the evil Count Dracula's cape, a London cinema tabloid, *To-Day's Cinema*, announced that Universal Studios had purchased the rights to Bram Stoker's *Dracula* to make it into a talking picture. The article further stated that, although the cast had not been picked, Conrad Veldt would play Count Dracula.

During the time Bela was cavorting under the stage spotlights as Count Dracula, he was also honing his talents as a screen actor. Though most of these films were mostly forgettable, Bela did keep a scrapbook of the "good" reviews. It was a practice he continued until he made the film *Dracula*, then he stopped.

In 1928, Bela Lugosi made his debut in *The Veiled Woman,* an Emmett Flynn production for Fox.

The following year, Bela had a prominent role in the film version of Corrine Griffith's *Prisoners,* directed by William Seitzer for First National. Also, he played the part of the inspector in *The Thirteenth Chair* for Metro-Goldwyn-Mayer.

In a departure from his dramatic roles, Bela played a mild-mannered singing teacher in the Fox production of *Oh, For A Man* in 1930.

Then, in 1931, Bela received the highest salary ever paid in the history of film. The *New York Telegraph* reported that Lugosi was paid $500 a minute for his part in Warner Brother's production of *Fifty Million Frenchmen.* In that film, Bela played an East Indian magician. The studio had to guarantee him one week's salary to get him to agree to play the part.

These films and several others, were the rungs Bela climbed on his way to reaching the top of the cinematic ladder and the role that would garner him the title of "legend."

CHAPTER THREE

DRACULA:
THE MAKING OF A LEGEND

I am a victim of the success of Dracula. *That horrible drama and, along with it, myself, have stumbled onto such great fame that producers and theater directors cannot even imagine that I could appear with a human face, too, and that I feel and believe that real art means talking with a human voice. I can't help it if they made a type out of me. The kind of role in which I have to work is completely foreign to my human and dramatic nature, but for the time being, I put up with my fate resignedly; I wear the clown's cap that I did not want at all.*

Now it does not even surprise me that my name and mysterious profile have infected the entire United States to such an extent that wherever I happen to be, from Hollywood to New York, even the smallest villages, friendly strangers call me by name. Anyway, that is my livelihood and I have to wait patiently for the days producers and theater directors to realize that, after all, I am a man too; someday I

will get back the old roles that I played before Dracula, or, at least, roles similar to them where I will be allowed to appear on the stage as a human being and speak with a human voice. Until then, I carry and bear this heavy cross.
Bela Lugosi on his fame from *Dracula* – August 17, 1933

In the Spring of 1887, a novel which would become the most cinematically translated work in literary history was born. From the mind of Bram Stoker came *Dracula*, the story of the undead. This novel popularized the spine-tingling word "VAMPIRE."

In November of 1847, Bram Stoker was born in Dublin, Ireland. Throughout his adolescence, he was an invalid. Because of his lack of physical ability, he learned to read at a very early age. He was usually observed with his nose in a book. While the young Bram Stoker buried his troubles in the Victorian fiction of his time, his imagination swelled. He then began to write short stories and novellas, though none of these was ever published.

At seven-and-a-half, Stoker took his first steps, which lead to an improvement in his health. His fragile physical condition was considered to have been more mental than physical. This is why it was believed that Stoker's medical condition improved because of his living in a fantasy world and bringing this "life" into his real world.

Stoker's career ambition of becoming a writer was thwarted until about 1875. Until then, he stayed in the literary field by working as a business writer for the municipality of Dublin, Ireland and by writing free-lance theatrical reviews for the newspaper, *The Dublin Mail*, in exchange for a byline.

Stoker was a natural as a fiction writer. He never gave up the art, no matter what physical or mental obstacles crossed his path. With this uppermost in his mind, at the age of 38, Stoker had his first piece in the horror genre published. It was a four part serialization of "The Chain of Destiny" in a Dublin newspaper. While writing this piece of fiction, Stoker was studying a topic which would make his one of the most famous names in horror . . . vampire.

In studying vampires, Stoker also began delving into the life of Vlad Tepes, known in the history books of the time as Vlad the Impaler. It was while researching the life and times of Vlad Tepes that Stoker added another possible title for the book he was thinking of writing to his list, *Dracula*. The titles he had previously written down were, *The Undead*

(Blank spaces indicate where the newspaper was to insert the date the film opened and the name of the theater.)

DRACULA STRANGE DRAMA
OF *UNDEAD*

An ancient superstition which claims that *undead* persons, hovering strangely between life and death, leave their grave on a certain night each year, forms the basis of *Dracula*, the hair-raising Universal drama which comes to the _____ theater on _____.

This old belief still persists in certain parts of Europe, and as the fateful night approaches abject terror seizes the peasants of the district, who cease all activities at sundown, and securely bolt all doors and windows. Wolves howl in the hills – and it is claimed that these animals are in reality human vampires who are able to change themselves at will into either wolves or bats, and thus gain access to places where a human being could not penetrate.

Count Dracula is the strange vampire of this startling story, and a trail of terror and death result from his horrible influence. The picture, it is said, has been produced with such sincerity and such artistry that the spectator is apt to forget for the moment that the story is what might be described as a glorified fairy tale, and to be completely carried away by the strange atmosphere of the play.

WEIRD SCENES IN
DRACULA VAMPIRE DRAMA

Fastnacht – the night of evil; swirling fog, and wolves howling in the mountain passes; a solitary traveler waiting at the cross-roads; the clatter of approaching hoofs, and a coachman with feverish eyes glowing above his great muffler.

The traveler enters the coach, which continues on its head-long flight; but as soon as it is again underway, the driver disappears, and his place is taken by a giant bat which flaps over the heads of the galloping horses. Silence settles over the misty landscape. The mysterious coach is swallowed up by dense fog, and makes its way to the crumbling castle of the terrible Count Dracula, vampire!

This is one of the opening scenes of *Dracula*, Universal's strange motion picture drama which was adapted from the stage success of the same name, and which comes to the _____ theater on _____.

ACTOR SHOULD CREATE HIS OWN CONCEPTION OF ROLE

Let the actor form his own conception of the actor he is to play!

This is the creed of Edward Van Sloan, the noted stage actor who makes his screen debut in *Dracula*, Universal's strange drama which comes to the _____ theater on

_____.

"I never want to know," says Van Sloan, "exactly how the playwright visualized the character which I am to play. In all my years on the stage, I have studiously avoided reading what he has to say on this subject, caring little whether he described him as a man with his hair cut pompadour, with or without glasses, or a mustache, or any of those little details which really mean nothing in arriving at a characterization. The actor has his own physical and temperamental limitations, and must be guided, it seems to me, by his own qualifications.

"Similarly, I have never read the book from which was made the stage adaptation of any play in which I have appeared. I did not want to be bound down by someone else's conception of a character which might conflict with my own, and thus perhaps be the means of developing a character which was neither one thing nor the other.

"On the stage I created the role of Dr. Van Helsing, and played the part for more than two years – but I have never read the book. Since I appeared in the play for almost a thousand performances, I, of course, became thoroughly acquainted with every move and inflection of the stage version, and I have now become almost as well acquainted with the screen play. But I must confess that there are many incidents about which I have only heard vaguely – incidents which appear in neither the stage or screen versions of this remarkable story."

DRACULA IS CROWNING SUCCESS OF DIRECTOR BROWNING'S CAREER

Tod Browning has carved a niche for himself as the motion picture industry's leading director of weird and fantastic crook stories.

It has been suggested that the dynamic Tod first obtained his idea of black magic, crooks and illusions in the carnival company with which he began his theatrical career, and in which he is said to have cut quite a figure as a contortionist. This was in 1908, when he was one of the principal attractions with *Willard and King's Great Traveling Show*.

Later Browning did a vaudeville act in blackface, after which he spent two years as principal comedian with a burlesque company known by the euphoric title of *The Whirl of Mirth*.

He made his screen debut in 1912, when he appeared as a slapstick comedian in a split-reel Biograph comedy directed by D. W. Griffith. This was followed by various roles of gradually ascending importance; and, in 1918, Browning became a full-fledged director, wielding the megaphone on *Which Woman*, a drama produced by Universal.

Among his important productions in the following years were such outstanding successes as *The Virgin of Stamboul, Under Two Flags, Outside the Law* and *The Thirteenth Chair*, as well as many of Lon Chaney's most successful pictures, such as *The Unholy Three, The Blackbird, The Unknown, The Road to Mandalay*. Browning's preference is for crook stories with a definite heart interest, and an example of his work along these lines is *Outside the Law,* which he wrote as well as directed.

Quite in line with his tendency towards mystery in many of his stories, Browning's favorite author is Conan Doyle, and he is an inveterate reader of the adventures of Sherlock Holmes. And still further along the line of this liking for mystery, the director is an enthusiastic amateur magician, and is one of the most adept prestidigitators in an industry which boasts many devotees of the art of magic.

What is said to be B owning's crowning efforts in the directorial field is *Dracula*, he weird screen drama adapted from Bram Stoker's strange n vel of the same name, and now at the _____ theater w h a cast headed by Bela Lugosi, the original Count Dracula of e stage play.

MASSIVE SETTIN IN *DRACULA* FILM

Some of the most picturesq e settings in the history of the screen are included in *Dracul* Universal's weird mystery which comes to the _____ theater on _____.

Many of the earlier scenes are la in and about the crumbling stone castle of Count Dracula, an a cient ruin which has been unoccupied for 500 years, except b Dracula and other "undead" vampires who return nightly fro n the grave and make of the castle a veritable home of horre s. Some of the most massive sets in the history of Hollywoo were constructed for this picture, showing various chambers an advanced state of disorder, with stone balustrades and pi s fallen into disordered ruins, and the entire interior festoor with cobwebs.

There are hair-raising scenes in a grave rd with a female vampire, risen from her grave, wandering disc solately among the tombstones. Opening sequences depict a pi turesque inn in the mountains of Transylvania, and a rocky mou tain pass on a foggy night, with wolves howling in the darkness.

After the story is transferred to England, involv g a terrible storm at sea, many scenes are laid in an ancient At ey leased by Dracula – a location which in its ruined constructio is greatly reminiscent of the castle in Transylvania.

Amid these picturesque settings is enacted what is   l to be the screen's strangest story, with the famous Bela Lugo n the title role of Count Dracula.

50 ENORMOUS BATS IN NEW MYSTERY FILM

Fifty enormous bats, those strange flapping creatures of the night, were recently taken to Universal City for use in a number of scenes of *Dracula*, the amazing drama which comes to the _____ theater on _____ with a cast which includes the famous Bela Lugosi, the original Dracula of the stage play.

The bats were captured in a great cave in Nevada by three residents of Las Vegas, who made an expedition into the nearby hill region when an emissary of Universal arrived in town with the strangest order ever delivered into the desert country.

It is interesting to note that for two months, Universal City qualified as the only place in the world where a large number of giant bats were being maintained in captivity.

HUMAN VAMPIRES ACTUALLY EXIST, U.S. HOSPITAL AUTHORITY DECLARES

Do human vampires actually exist?

Records of the United States government say that they do. In fact, Dr. John E. Lind, physician in charge of Howard Hall, the hospital for the criminal insane at the St. Elizabeth's Hospital, the Federal Institution at Washington, D.C., is authority for the statement that for many years a vampire has been one of the inmates – a sailor.

Thus a measure of credibility is given to *Dracula*, Universal's strange drama based on Bram Stoker's famous novel, and scheduled to open in an engagement at the _____ theater on _____.

Count Dracula, the central character of the story, is a vampire, and his attacks on other persons in the story are the means of forcing them, too, into the terrible legion of the "undead."

GIGANTIC COBWEBS BUILT FOR PICTURE

The world's largest spider web, a great filmy fabric 18 feet in diameter, is seen in *Dracula*, Universal's strange vampire drama which comes to the _____ theater on _____.

This gigantic cobweb entirely fills the grand stairway in the ancient stone castle of Count Dracula – hundreds of years old, which has fallen into ruin and decay.

And it is through this giant web that Dracula, vampire, walks at will without harming it.

The construction of this artificial cobweb is most interesting, illustrating as it does the uncanny artistry of studio technical departments. After long experimenting is found that rubber cement, if drawn out to filmy fineness, exactly simulated cobwebs, and there remained only the necessity of finding some method of reducing the sticky material to the form of delicate threads. This finally brought about the invention of a sort of rotary gun electrically operated, which expels the cement in such a filmy form that it is almost invisible as it comes out. The magazine having been filled with rubber cement, then it is only necessary for the operator to turn on the current, point the gun at the desired spot, and within a few seconds an apparently genuine cobweb begins to form.

Though this entire set in the picture is festooned with cobwebs, in only this largest one was it necessary to construct an artificial framework on which to hang the filmy threads.

BELA LUGOSI, FAMOUS ACTOR, TELLS OF TERRIBLE EXPERIENCE WITH ACTUAL HUMAN VAMPIRE

The strangest creature in America is living today in Hollywood, surrounded by a brooding atmosphere of horror and madness. A tall, straight figure of a man, he goes among his

emotions of the audience – which, perhaps, is a compliment to the artistry with which the film was produced.

Scenically, *Dracula* is magnificent, and its settings fully preserve the thrillingly uncanny atmosphere of the story.

The title role of Count Dracula is played with remarkable respect by Bela Lugosi, who created the same part in the stage play, and who delivers an arresting performance as the sinister vampire who is the central character of the story. Helen Chandler is altogether charming and capable in the principal feminine part, and David Manners, as her fiance, does the type of work which has made him one of the most popular leading men.

THEY ALWAYS GASP WHEN THEY MEET BELA LUGOSI, STAR OF *DRACULA*

They always gasp when they meet Bela Lugosi! For years Lugosi played on the stage a sinister vampire, Count Dracula, in the stage play of *Dracula* and the character was maintained at such a high pitch of dramatic intensity that he came to be looked upon by theater-goers as really a strange being of the most horrible description. This reputation clung to him outside the theater, since the artistry of his performance created an effect on the audience that was not dissipated at the close of the performance.

And so when the actor was presented socially to some person, either male or female, there always came that little catch in the throat, and some such exclamation as, "Oh, you're Dracula."

The polished, kindly gentleman, smiling his shy, warm smile, has ceased to be surprised at such a reception, but he is inclined to regret it a tiny bit.

"Always they gasp!," he says with his slight Hungarian accent. "For a few moments they fear me a little, I think, but soon I think, too, that they begin to like me. I want them to, because, really, I am only bad when I have my makeup on."

FANDUS SCIENTIST IN *DRACULA* BESIEGED WITH STRANGE QUERIES

"How long does a soul live after death! What is the secret of the apparently genuine visitations from my sister, who has been dead for more than forty years!"

This is the sort of question that has been continually asked of Edward Van Sloan during the past three years, and all because he has been playing the role of the scientific Dr. Van Helsing in the weird stage play, *Dracula*, which has just been made into a motion picture by Universal and which comes to the _____ theater on _____. Depicted thus as a learned scientist, he has been bombarded with a constant stream of letters which give him credit for the occult knowledge of these things about which human beings really know nothing, and he has been at considerable pains to acquit himself according to the ideas of those who know him in his fictitious character of Van Helsing, and not in his true persona of Van Sloan.

"I appreciate the confidence of those who have written to me in the past three years," says Van Sloan. "Surely one could do no less. But the reason that I have not attempted to offer any solutions of the many problems which have been presented to me is simply this: I just did not know! I have been merely an actor playing a part, and while I have gone somewhat deeply into the subject of my role, I have been groping, as have many members of my audience, in an attempt to find a solution of many of life's strange and perplexing problems.

"And now that I am appearing as the same scientific doctor in the screen version of *Dracula*, I suppose that my [and rather particular type of fan] mail will show a great disconcerting increase."

BELA LUGOSI HAUNTED BY THE ROLE HE MADE FAMOUS IN *DRACULA*

One of the most famous of all actors on stage or screen would like to forget the character that made him famous! Audiences on Broadway were thrilled for more than two years by his artistry; millions of picture fans throughout the country are being fascinated by the startling impersonation he gives on the screen. But the character haunts him, and he never wants to play it again.

The actor is Bela Lugosi, and the character is Count Dracula in the most startling of all plays or pictures – *Dracula*. Bram Stoker, the famous English novelist, wrote it first as a novel – this terrifying narration of an "undead" being who rises from his grave at night and through his horrible influence brings death and suffering to his victims.

For more than a thousand nights, Lugosi played it in the theater. Then when the Universal Studios decided to produce the great story as a picture, Lugosi was the natural choice for the role he made so famous on the stage.

At first it was difficult to prevail upon him to appear on the screen. He had lived with the horrible vampire character so long on the stage that he wanted to forget, and how could he forget if he played it again on the screen.

But he finally consented and for weeks at the Universal City studios while the picture was in production, he lived again the startling fantastic role of Count Dracula. Those who have seen both play and picture assert that his impersonation for the film is even greater than his stage work.

But now that the picture is finished and shortly to be shown at the theater, Lugosi says he will never play the role again.

And Lugosi's determination is in itself a great tribute to his ability as an actor. If he had been able to act the part mechanically – had not thrown himself heart-and-soul into the role – it would not have the terrors that it now has. But a great artist does not play mechanically, and Lugosi is a great artist. Thus each night in the theater and for many days at the picture studios, his nervous system has been subjected to terrible strain.

DRACULA CAUSES SENSATION AMONG PICTURE GOERS

The entire city is gasping over *Dracula*, Universal's strange drama which closes its run at the _____ theater on _____ night, and which has created a veritable sensation among local theater goers.

Never before, it is said, has the screen presented a story which exercises such a powerful effect on the emotions of the audience dealing as it does with the terrible depredations of a human vampire and his steadily mounting influence over the very lives of a group of people, combated by the apparently hopeless efforts of a scientific physician.

Bela Lugosi, the famous Hungarian actor, is seen in the title role.

LUGOSI AT HIGH EMOTIONAL PITCH IN *DRACULA* ROLE

Bela Lugosi never did learn to play Dracula mechanically. The famous Hungarian actor was starred in this strange play for more than two years, and during all that time he was worked up to a high pitch of emotional intensity which actually had a devastating effect on his health.

"After I had been in the play for a month," said Lugosi recently, "I began to 'take stock of myself,' and I realized that for my own well-being I should make some attempt to conserve my mental and physical strength – to throw myself with less fervor into the depiction of the role. By that time I knew every inflection, every movement, every expression required of the character, and I decided that if I could go through the play somewhat mechanically – somewhat more placidly within myself – there would be no lessening of the effect on my performance on the audience, but a decided lessening of the effect on my own nervous system.

"But I could not do it. The role seemed to demand that I keep myself worked up to a fever pitch, and so I sat in my dressing room and took on, as nearly as possible, the actual attributes of the horrible vampire, Dracula. And during all those two years I did not speak a word to any person behind the scenes during the progress of the play. And, since everyone knew the strain I was laboring under, no one spoke to me. When I came off the stage after a scene I went silently to my dressing room, and did not emerge until it was again time for me to go on the stage. I was under a veritable spell which I dared not break. If I stepped out of my character for even a moment, the seething menace of the terrible Count Dracula was gone from the characterization, and my hold on the audience lost its force."

DRACULA CREATES FUROR AMONG PICTURE FANS

_____ night marks the close of the engagement of *Dracula*, Universal's uncanny mystery drama which has been creating a veritable sensation at the _____ theater.

No other talking picture ever shown in (your city) has created such a furor of comment, or has so powerfully gripped the emotions of local theater-goers. The strange subject of this startling picture – the nightly prowlings of "undead" human vampires – brings an entirely new note to the screen, and forms the basis of a story which is filled with the weird atmosphere of the supernatural.

Though not a part of the studio publicity for *Dracula*, the studio did distribute the following transcript to newspapers and movie magazines to promote the film.

This is an exact transcript of a speech Bela Lugosi gave on March 27, 1931, over the airwaves of radio station KFI in Los Angeles to promote the opening of *Dracula*. The grammar, spelling and punctuation are those of Bela Lugosi.

I read the book, *Dracula*, written by Bram Stoker, 18 years ago, and I always dreamed to create and to play the part of Dracula. Finally the opportunity came. Horace Liveright, stage producer of New York, acquired the stage rights of the novel and he chose me for the part. I have played the role of Dracula about a thousand times on the stage, and people often ask me if I still retain my interest in the character. I do intensely. Because many people regard the story of *Dracula* simply as a glorified superstition, the actor who plays the role is constantly engaged in the battle of wits with the audience, in a sense, since he is constantly striving to make the character so real that the audience will believe in it.

Now that I have appeared in the screen version of the story which Universal has just completed, I am of course not under this daily strain in the depiction of the character. My work in this direction was finished with the completion of the picture, but while it was being made I was working more intensely to this end than I ever did on the stage.

Although *Dracula* is a fanciful tale of a fictional character, it is actually a story which has many essential elements of truth. I was born and reared in almost the exact location of the story, and I came to know that what is looked upon merely as a superstition of ignorant people, is really based on facts which are literally hair-raising in their strangeness – but which are true. Many people will leave the theater with a sniff at the fantastic character of the story, but many others who think just as deeply will gain an insight into one of the most remarkable facts of human existence.

Dracula is a story which has always had a powerful effect on the emotions of an audience, and I think that the picture will be no less effective than the stage play. In fact, the motion picture should even prove more remarkable in this direction, since many things which could only be talked about on the stage are shown on the screen in all their uncanny detail.

I am sure you will enjoy *Dracula*. I am sure you will be mightily affected by its strange story, and I hope that it will make you think – about the weirdest, most remarkable condition that ever affected mankind.

I thank you.

The huge publicity push put on by Universal Studios for *Dracula* worked in a big way. The film went on to be one of the highest grossing films of its era. And, as time has proven, a classic of the horror genre (though the word "horror" was not associated with the film during its initial run in the theaters).

Although Universal's publicity made it seem like everything was perfect in this film version of Bram Stoker's classic novel, in actuality, it was not. The first problem was who would play the title role of Count Dracula? In reference to this question, history has given us many suppositions. Bela Lugosi was the first choice to play the part.

Once Universal Studios decided to do a film production of *Dracula*, the studio moguls lined up and signed all of the behind-the-camera technicians. When this was done, they drew up a list of actors to be considered for the title role of Count Dracula. This list included Bela Lugosi, Conrad Veldt, Lon Chaney, William Courtney, Paul Muni, and Ian Keith.

Many film historians have written that the first choice for the Satanic Count was Lon Chaney. There is no doubt that Universal would have loved Lon Chaney to play Count Dracula because Chaney's name on a theater marquee guaranteed big box office receipts. However, Chaney was suffering from throat cancer at the time of the casting. The only reason Chaney's name appeared on Universal's list was out of respect for the actor and the respect for director of *Dracula,* Ted Browning. (Browning directed Chaney in many films which, by popular consensus, were considered Chaney's best works).

Paul Muni's name appeared on the list only because of his current popularity, which made his association with the film good publicity.

Conrad Veldt, an impeccable actor with incredible acting depth, was also a serious consideration for the lead role. After finding out the film's plot, he informed everyone involved that he was not interested; he felt that it was unworthy of his talents.

So, "Why Bela Lugosi as Dracula?" To answer this question, it helps to put yourself in the shoes of the moguls at Universal Studios.

Bela Lugosi had gained national recognition for his portrayal of the deadly Count on stage – from New York to San Francisco. So, those in charge of the purse strings at Universal knew that the public would be able to relate to Bela's portrayal. They also knew that Bela was even better known in Europe for his dramatic talents. So, there would be a large audience waiting for the film across the Atlantic – meaning still more money for the studio. Although all these reasons are sound and make great business sense, none of these are the main reason why Bela Lugosi was awarded the role, which made him an icon of the horror cinema.

The bottom line of filmmaking is money and Bela was chosen because he would come cheap. The grand sum he received from the film amounted to five thousand dollars. It is interesting to note Universal did not consider that Bela was from Transylvania, had an genuine Count Dracula accent, and looked remarkably like some of the paintings of Vlad the Impaler. Although, Universal did take advantage of these attributes for publicity purposes.

Once the feature roles for *Dracula* were cast, one other important person needed to be chosen, the film's director. Tod Browning was the first choice, but in order to get Browning, Universal Pictures had to pay a large sum of money. Browning had a great track record with horror films; all were silent films starring Lon Chaney, who had a penchant for the "dark side." This is why Universal did not balk at Browning's salary demands (which have never been divulged).

Tod Browning was indeed a film director who lived the adage, "life imitates art." Although in this case, the wording could have been reversed to "art imitates life." Browning's real name was Charles Albert Browning; he changed it to Tod when he ran away from home at 16. When Browning ran away, like a character out of a juvenile novel, he joined Ringling Brother's Circus. He performed the usual circus chores, cleaning up animal waste and working as a "gofer," which soon landed him a job as a clown. (This was before Ringling joined forces with its main circus competitor, Barnum and Bailey.)

After Browning tired of the greasepaint smile, shocking wigs, and shoes 10 sizes too large for his feet, he left the circus to take on a new "sideshow" career as a freak, "The Living Hypnotic Corpse."

The circus and sideshows gave Browning his first taste of show business. He then took the next logical show-business step; he decided to try his hand at a new entertainment medium, the cinema. In choosing a filmmaking teacher to tutor him, Browning was fortunate enough to latch on to the "Father of American Filmmaking," the legendary D. W. (David Warwick) Griffith. Under Griffith's tutelage, Browning mastered the craft of filmmaking. This mastery, combined with his penchant for portraying humanity's darkside, soon made him one of the hottest directors of his time.

In Hollywood's "Golden Era," many directors formed teams with actors and Tod Browning was no exception. He usually associated with the immortal Lon Chaney, "Man of a Thousand Faces." The last 10 films Chaney starred in, all considered classics, were directed by Tod Browning.

It is because of this "horrific" teaming and his style of filmmaking, that the following was written about Browning: The natural residence of

Figure 3 – Lon Chaney is often said to have been the first choice to play Dracula. This may or may not be true. Chaney died before the script was even completed. Lugosi, after portraying Dracula, was considered to be Chaney's heir to the throne as the King of Horror. (Copyright © 1927 by Universal Studios, Inc. Courtesy of MCA Publishing Rights, a Division of MCA Inc. All Rights Reserved)

Browning's psyche was an attic, a crypt, a closet, a coffin, a shadow, a staircase, a trunk; it was terrorized by sunlight, fields, deserts, woods and open spaces. That terror became his style and strength. In succeeding films, his anxieties drove him further into the shadows. Tod Browning was the agoraphobic director par excellence.

Although Browning worked with Bela Lugosi on a couple of films (Browning's first "talkie," *The Thirteenth Chair,*1929). This actor/ director relationship will always be best known for the 1931 film adaptation of Bram Stoker's *Dracula.* This film not only ushered in the American horror genre, but it is also one of the most influential films to ever come out of Hollywood.

Tod Browning was usually remembered for making *Dracula,* but film historians and cinema buffs remember him best for the film *Freaks,* which has become a cult classic. When Browning made this film, he went back to his entertainment roots, the circus sideshows, to create such a perversely realistic film of actual circus freaks. *Freaks* was not only banned worldwide, Metro-Goldwyn-Mayer also removed its name from all prints, which included its logo and Leo, the ever-present roaring lion. Thirty years after *Freaks* was banned, it reemerged in art-house theaters where a whole new generation of film reviewers and critics gave it rave reviews (although very few have seen the unedited version in which a knife-wielding dwarf castrates a man).

Tod Browning succumbed to cancer of the larynx and a stroke on October 6, 1962.

As it was with all of Tod Browning films, he demanded, and always received, the right to rework the script he was directing. *Dracula* was no exception. However, being the creature of habit he was, Browning was reworking the script without his star, Bela Lugosi, in mind.

Browning's business relationship with Lon Chaney was as close as any director/star relationship in Hollywood history. The majority of Browning films, up until this point, had starred Chaney. Browning was used to reworking films to fit the talents of Lon Chaney. Chaney died just before Browning reworked the *Dracula* script. Chaney was on Browning's mind while developing the Dracula lead, instead of Lugosi (even though Lugosi and Browning had worked together before *Dracula*). It was not until the initial script read-through by the stars that Browning realized it was all wrong for Lugosi. He had, eerily enough, written the lead as if Chaney were going to come back from the dead to play the part. When

Browning realized the error of his artistic ways, he once again re-worked the script, which created the film *Dracula,* as we all know it.

In the final draft of *Dracula* (it went through four drafts before the final one was shot.), the role of Count Dracula was lessened considerably. For instance, Bela Lugosi speaks only 77 lines, consisting of 621 words (averaging only nine words per line). This is truly incredible since Bela was the star of the film and Dracula was, obviously, the focus of the film.

There is a simple reason why Browning reduced Lugosi's speaking role; Bela's command of the English language was minimal and there were certain words Bela just could not pronounce well enough for them to be understood. Of course, Bela took full advantage of his speaking parts by saying them slowly and deliberately. For instance, it took Bela five seconds to say one of the films most famous lines: "I am Dracula" (the word "Dracula" Bela makes into three separate words Dra-Cu-La).

Browning's final working of the *Dracula* script, as history has proven, has given us the following memorable lines:

"I am Dracula."

"The walls of my castle are broken – the shadows are many – but come, I bid you welcome."

"Listen to them – the children of the night! What music they make."

"The eternal struggle for life – each living creature must have blood to live. The spider, spinning his web for the unwary fly . . ."

"I never drink – wine."

"To die – to be really dead, that must be glorious."

"There are far worse things awaiting man – than death."

"For one who has not lived even a single lifetime, you're a wise man."

It is the Lugosi portrayal of the evil Count that hypnotizes those who view the film. However, Karl Freund, the film's cinematographer and its future film director, emerges as the real star. The reason the 1931 version of *Dracula* is still popular today on video, is not only because of Bela Lugosi's performance, but also because of the film's "darkness," the way it was filmed in shadows. Today's cinematographers refer to this as its "starkness."

Karl Freund's vision for this film is evident from the first scenes to the last. It is his mind which brought to life the film's opening, where Renfield

(Dwight Frye) travels through the Caspian Mountains to Castle Dracula. Renfield comes to a small village where the residents try to warn him of the evil he is about to encounter. Freund was looking for an atmosphere which would grab the audience's mind and not let go for the next 80-plus minutes. Did Freund succeed in his visionary quest? The answer lies in the success of this film.

Once the carriage transporting Renfield climbs the Borga Pass, enroute to Castle Dracula, the viewers get their first glimpse of Dracula's "home of the undead." To capture this breathtaking view, Karl Freund once again put his masterful, artistic mind to work. Because the film was shot on a Universal lot in Los Angeles, there were no castles available to shoot. For that matter, there were also no mountains which could even come close to representing the awesome Carpathian Mountain range.

To achieve the desired look for this scene, Karl Freund used a picture of the Rocky Mountains as a backdrop and placed a model of a castle in front of it. The model was based on a photograph of a European castle – not the original abode of Vlad the Impaler. This model took 24 hours to build and cost Universal Pictures $2,000 to erect, and stood an imposing five feet high.

For the castle's interior shots, Freund wanted, and located, a massive set. To achieve the dramatic shadows, Karl Freund wanted everything to look enormous surrounding the imposing form of Bela Lugosi. The interior set of the castle almost filled one entire soundstage from floor-to-ceiling. David Manners, who portrayed Jonathan Harker in *Dracula*, remembers the set:

> In the finished film, the height of this set was extended to Westminster-like proportions through the use of a painting on glass mounted in front of the camera.

Of course, the most remembered sight of the castle's interior is the huge spider web on the set's massive staircase. This spider web measured 18 feet in diameter. To achieve a spider web of this size, Freund first used a "spider web gun," a machine used in carnival haunted houses. Although the machine worked perfectly, the spider web did not show up on film the vivid detail Freund was looking for. After trying numerous other methods to no avail, Freund had his crew shoot rubber cement through a rotary gun to form the spider web. It not only worked well, but it also filmed perfectly.

Another interior shot called for the use of armadillos scampering around the castle's first floor. As the story goes, Freund was looking at a book on rodents to determine which would be the best to have running around the castle. When he saw the pictures of the armadillos (Freund was relatively new to America from Germany and had never seen such a creature) they reminded him of prehistoric creatures. Freund felt this would be good for the film. He was apparently correct because not one reviewer or critic mentioned that armadillos were running around a castle in Transylvania – an area where they do not exist.

The most important (and, as it would turn out, most famous) thing that Karl Freund did for the film was the way he focused lighting on Bela as Count Dracula. As cinema fans will remember, Dracula hypnotizes his victims before he takes their blood. To show the cinematic audience that the victims were being hypnotized, Freund focused two penlights on Bela's eyes, giving them an hypnotic stare. However, not everything went as planned.

For reasons unexplained, the penlight's focus on Bela's eyes was off-center. One light caught one eye directly on-center, while the other light veered off, which Freund had not intended. The effect went beyond a hypnotic stare to the point of being downright scary. Because of this error in artistic judgment, the eyes of Bela Lugosi became the most famous in the history of the cinema. Beginning with *Dracula*, whenever Bela portrayed a "bad guy," his eyes were the central part of the character.

When *Dracula* finally received the go-ahead to begin filming, director Tod Browning was given a budget of $350,000 and seven weeks to complete the film. According to today's standards, this would seem an impossible task; but 1931 was an era in filmmaking when money meant something and time was of the essence.

When *Dracula* was filmed, the filmmaking process of dubbing had not yet been introduced. Today's post-production dubbing remedies an actor misreading his lines. Both Lugosi as Dracula and Edward Van Sloan as Van Helsing reenacted their roles from the Broadway stage. They knew their character's physical movements and, as stage actors, quickly memorized their lines (although an error in Bela's speech would be hard to pick up because of his thick Hungarian accent).

All went well during the actual filming of *Dracula*; but, there was one point when Tod Browning almost pulled out what little hair he had. The concert hall set, where Dracula meets the central cast members at the symphony in London, did not photograph well. After throwing a temper tantrum because this setback the filming schedule, Browning turned to Karl Freund and said, "Dammit! Do something!" Freund did do something.

Within a matter of hours, the cast and a smiling Tod Browning were on *The Phantom of the Opera* soundstage. The stage where Lon Chaney had mesmerized audiences in 1925. Fruend turned this set into London's acclaimed Albert Hall and filmed the scene.

After about three weeks of filming, Bela Lugosi transformed into a real-life monster. The cause of this transformation was his own fault.

Because Bela wanted the role of Dracula so badly, he essentially sold his financial soul to the devil. Even though he was the film's star, he was the least paid of the central characters. Bela received only $3,500 for seven weeks of work. At that time, there was no such thing as "a percentage of the box office." On the other side of the cinematic coin, David Manners, who portrayed Jonathan Harker, was paid $2,000 a week for the entire time spent filming *Dracula*. When Bela realized that he was on the low end of the pay scale, he distanced himself from the other cast members. He began to detest the one word which would make him a legend – Dracula!

Bela's aloofness toward his fellow cast members was best summed up by David Manners who remembers:

> I mainly remember Lugosi standing in front of a full-length mirror between scenes, intoning "I am Dracula." He was mysterious and never really said anything to the other members of the cast except good morning when he arrived and good night when he left. He was polite, but always distant. He was a vain and eccentric performer, though I never thought he was acting, but being the odd man he was.

For most of the filming of *Dracula*, Bela's "monstrous" ways remained on the set. Once word reached the cinematic tabloids, however, it was as if Bela had turned into a bloody piece of meat set adrift in a pool of sharks. On August 23, 1930, *Filmograph Magazine* screamed, "Bela should be given the role of Dracula." It reported in their October 10, 1930, edition:

> So horrible is this grotesque monster that everyone on the Big U [Universal] lot is terrified whenever Bela Lugosi emerges

Figure 4 – Bela in character, in front of filmdom's most famous prop, the larger-than-life spider web produced by shooting rubber cement from a special gun. (Copyright © 1931 by Universal Studios, Inc. Courtesy of MCA Publishing Rights, a Division of MCA Inc. All Rights Reserved)

from his dressing room . . . . Child prodigies scamper into prop rooms . . . even hard-riding cowboys stand at the head of their trembling steeds.

Even the most popular of the cinematic tabloids began reporting on Bela's "problems." After visiting Lugosi on the set of *Dracula*, journalist Lillian Shirley reported in the March 1931 issue of *Modern Screen* that the actor had reached the point of actually hating both the part and the character. She wrote:

> I was with him when a telegram arrived. It was from Henry Duffy, the Pacific Coast theater impresario, who wanted Mr. Lugosi to play Dracula for 16 weeks. Lugosi threw down the message in disgust, his face visibly reddening, even beneath the gray-green makeup. "No! Not at any price! When I am through with this picture I hope never to hear of Dracula again! I cannot stand it . . . . I do not intend that it shall possess me. No one knows what I suffer from this role."

Two years after the name Bela Lugosi became synonymous with Dracula, he gave an interview to *Ez Ember* (an Hungarian newspaper in New York City) where he talked about his portrayal of the evil, blood-sucking Count.

> I am a victim of the success of *Dracula*. That horror drama and, along with it, myself, have stumbled onto such great fame that producers and theater directors cannot even imagine that I could appear with a human face, too, and that I feel and believe that real art means talking with a human voice. I can't help it if they make a type out of me. The kind of role in which I have to work is completely foreign to my human and dramatic nature, but, for the time being, I put up with my fate resignedly; I wear the clown's cap that I did not want at all.
> Now it does not even surprise me that my name and mysterious profile have infected the entire United States to such an extent that wherever I happen to be, from Hollywood to New York, even in the smallest villages, friendly strangers call me by name. Anyway, that is my livelihood and I have to wait patiently for the day that producers and theater directors realize that,

after all, I am a man too; someday, I will get back to the old roles that I played before Dracula, or, at least, roles similar to them where I will be allowed to appear on the stage as a human being and speak with a human voice. Until then, I carry and bear this heavy cross.

Although Bela Lugosi disagreed with his treatment as the star of *Dracula* and was tiring of the role (after playing it for so long on stage and now on film), he found it to be a learning experience. In an interview with *Filmograph* magazine on October 18, 1930, Bela discussed the making of *Dracula*:

> In playing in the picture [*Dracula*] I found that there was a great deal that I had to unlearn. In the theater I was playing not only to the spectators in the front rows but also to those in the last row of the gallery, and there was some exaggeration in everything I did, not only in the tonal pitch of my voice but in the changes of the facial expression which accompanied various lines or situations, as was necessary.
>
> But for the screen, in which the actors' distance from every member of the audience is equal only to his distance from the lens of the camera, I have found that a great deal of repression was an absolute necessity. Tod Browning has continually had to "hold me down." In my other screen roles, I did not seem to have this difficulty; but, I have played Dracula a thousand times on the stage and, in this role, I find that I have been thoroughly settled in the technique of the stage and not of the screen. But, thanks to director Browning, I am unlearning fast.

Bela Lugosi was not the only one going through a metamorphosis; so was Universal Studios. Not only was *Dracula* the first horror sound film, it was also the first horror film to be given a budget which resembled, in a minor way, that of a typical studio feature film. Universal was taking a gamble; and, according to the moguls at the competing studios, it was a gamble which favored failure.

During Hollywood's Golden Era (the 20's through the 40's), before a script went before the cameras, the script had to go through a panel of "readers." The job of these readers was to determine whether the script could be made into a profitable film (surprisingly enough, the readers were right most of the time). As far as the film *Dracula* was concerned, the readers had both the script and play to look at in their collective effort to determine its cinematic profitability. For the most part, they were not convinced.

The following are a few of the memos written by the readers about the making of *Dracula* the feature film:

> This is, without a doubt, one of the most horrible, gruesome stories that has ever been written. For a picture, it is out of the question . . . mostly because of censorship. The first part of the story could be shown, but from the moment you take up the part of Lucy, you run into all sorts of difficulties.

> For years the picture people have been trying to find a way of doing this thing on screen; and, so far, have never succeeded, nor have they had the nerve to try it, after they have analyzed what they can and cannot put of it on the screen or in the story adaptation. It might be a novelty – but would it pay in the end?

> Were this story put on the screen, it would be an insult to every one of its audience. We all like to see ugly things . . . (for instance the big appeal of *The Phantom of the Opera*). But when it passes a certain point, the attraction dies and we suffer a feeling of repulsion and nausea. This story certainly passes beyond the point of what the average person can stand or cares to stand.

> *Dracula* is and always has been material for a great picture, great in opportunity for actors, writers, and directors. Great in opportunity for photography of a wonderful sort and nature. Although, it is picture material from the angle of the pictorial and the dramatic, it is not picture material from the standpoint of the box office nor of ethics of the industry. It would be a thing which no child and for that matter, no adult of delicate nervous temperament should see, a thing beside which *The Cabinet of Dr. Caligari* would seem like a pleasant fireside reverie.

> For mystery and bloodcurdling horror, I have never read its equal. For sets, impressionistic and weird, it cannot be sur-

passed. This story contains everything necessary for a weird, unnatural, mysterious picture.

It is usually the case that if a story can be played upon the stage, a screen version can be written from it as well. It will be a difficult task; and, one will run up against the censor continually; but, I think it can be done. It is daring; but, if done, there can be no doubt as to its making money.

History has proven all but the last reader to be quite wrong. It is interesting, however, to note the word "censorship" in a few of the inner-studio memos. It is this worry of censorship which, in many film historians' mind, has made *Dracula* the film classic it is today.

Because of the censorship worries, *Dracula* became more of a psychological horror film (compared to the blood-and-guts slasher films of today). Nowhere in the film does the viewer see blood or Dracula actually put his mouth upon a victim's body (thus no fangs puncture necks). What is seen is the Count's hypnotic stare, his mind control of the victims, and his utter manageability of the task which lay before him. Actually, from its literal point, it is more of a macabre love story than a story of horror (this is not the case in the myriad versions which have followed).

The aura of romance did not elude those in power at Universal Pictures. Before the film was released, theatrically, the original trailers were to promote the romantic aspects of the film. Whether, Universal was hoping for a larger audience with the romantic twist of the film or it was concerned that "horror" would not play well at the box office, is still a matter of controversy among film historians.

One of the Hollywood myths which has surrounded *Dracula* and its romanticism is associated with the film's opening at New York City's Roxy Theater on Valentine's Day in 1931. The myth is that Universal Pictures chose this day to reiterate the film's romantic aura. There is no validity to this conjecture.

The actual reason the film had its world premiere on Valentine's Day was because the original opening date was Friday, February 13. When the film's director, Tod Browning, heard of the Friday-the-thirteenth opening, he took an unprecedented move and sent the following telegram to the owner of the Roxy Theater:

> Dear Roxy don't blame me but I was born superstitious stop Just heard you are opening *Dracula* Friday stop That's bad enough but Friday the thirteenth is terrible stop I have put everything I have into this picture and as a favor to me can't you open your presentation Thursday stop
> Best Regards
> Tod Browning

To please Browning, Universal gave into Browning's superstitious concerns and changed the opening a day, not to Thursday the 12th as Browning had suggested, but to Saturday the 14th, Valentine's Day.

With the early publicity *Dracula* received and the trailers (coming attractions) which preceded its opening, the box office response was tremendous. Unlike the film openings of today, *Dracula* did not open nationwide on the same day. After its initial viewing at the Roxy Theater in New York City, it opened nationwide in waves. *Dracula* finally made its West Coast premiere in late March, 1931. With each opening, the reviews were mixed; but, the universal audience reaction to the film was shock. In various theaters, movie goers passed out, ran from the theater in utter fright or screamed themselves hoarse. It finally got to the point where Universal Pictures placed registered nurses in the theater lobbies, a ploy Universal used to publicize the film even more.

Dracula was a major hit; and, the cinematic genre of horror was born. By the end of the year, *Dracula* had become Universal Pictures biggest grossing picture to this day.

Quite possibly, the most significant thing to come from this classic film is that Bela Lugosi became one of Hollywood's major sex symbols. Becoming a sex symbol in Hollywood, at that time, was not a major feat for a young, dashing actor – but, Bela Lugosi was 50 years old. Bela commented on sex symbol status:

> It is women who love horror. They hoped that I was Dracula. They hoped that my love was the love of Dracula. It is the embrace of death their subconscious is yearning for. Death, the final triumphant of love.

In the Hollywood of today, there is a saying which goes: "Fame is fleeting. You're hot today and cold tomorrow." This was not the case for Bela Lugosi. Fame was not fleeting; it was stagnant. His portrayal of

Dracula left such an impression on the audience that it could not be broken.

It is obvious by now, Bela Lugosi felt the cinematic wrath, which some actors experience, toward what is known in the film industry as "typecasting." But, Bela didn't realize this until 1934, three years after his immortal portrayal. Bela once noted in an interview:

> A strange thing happened to me following *Dracula*. I discovered that every producer in Hollywood had definitely set me down as a "type" – an actor of this particular kind of role. Considering that before *Dracula*, I had never, in a long time and varied career on the stage of two continents, played anything but leads and straight characters. I was both amused and disappointed.
>
> Of course, it is true that every actor's greatest ambition is to create his own definite and original role – a character with which he will always be identified. But on the screen, I found this to be almost fatal. It took me years to live down Dracula and convince the film producers that I would play almost any other type of role.

It is interesting to note that he never did "live down Dracula."

Much has been written about Bela Lugosi's immortal portrayal of Count Dracula. When it came to dissecting his portrayal, actress Carrol Borland (Bela's co-star in *Mark of the Vampire*) said it best. The following quotations are from an interview Borland gave to author and film historian Richard Bojarski for his 1980 book, *The Films of Bela Lugosi*:

> Let me admit with no apology that, to me, Dracula is Bela Lugosi; and, Lugosi is Dracula. There is no separation of the two. Many have donned his nocturnal cloak, and some, like Christopher Lee, have presented most credible representations of the great undead Count – but, can never be Dracula. If not for technicolor, I could say they are only pale imitations.
>
> In saying that Dracula is Lugosi's creation, I do not denigrate the original character contribution of Bram Stoker. But in recalling the evil Count of Stoker's novel – seamed revolting face, hooked nose, long drooping mustache, small, ember-lit eyes

under craggy brows – his is a visage more rightly ascribed to the fierce Genghis Khan or Arpad, the Hun.

Dracula embodied by Lugosi is suave, debonair and fascinating, from the sleek dark hair of the "Latin Lover" movie idol of the period, to the tips of his elegant opera pumps. The Satanic face, arched to a pointed widow's peak, aquiline nose, eyes of blue flame – like the disturbing note in the creamy mask of a Siamese cat – the dark circumflex of brows, all in a stunning contrast with the sensual features of the pouting, bowed mouth, and provocatively cleft oval chin.

This physical dichotomy emphasizes the important difference between Lugosi's Dracula and those who have imitated him. No other actor has succeeded in including that subtle appeal which made his vampire portrayal so dreadful that one was both attracted and repelled, loathing, yet forced to love. Is this not the ultimate horror? Lugosi needed no superficial fangs, claws or bloody teeth. His victims willingly gave themselves to discover the dreadful consummation achieved behind the swirling, concealing cloak. Modern films, replete with naive explicitness, can never rival the ultimate suggested horror.

Some agree with the psychological thesis that Count Dracula is a death figure, and that we all have a secret death wish. To many, women in particular, the vampire incarnated that great unknown factor. He was stronger than other men, supremely powerful and most feared. For women, guardians and carriers of life, Dracula is the dark enigma whom they can conquer only by being conquered. Death, as Count Dracula, is potent, brooding and bristling with a perverse vitality exemplifying the undefeatable power of the Undead.

At the end of the original version of *Dracula* (and on the new home video editions), this speech was given by Edward Van Sloan in the persona of Dr. Van Helsing. The scene was eventually cut because theatergoers took it both literally and seriously.

Please! One Moment!
Just a word before you go. We hope the memories of Dracula won't give you bad dreams – so just a word of reassurance! When you get home tonight and the lights have

been turned out and you're afraid to look behind the curtains –
and you dread to see a face appear at the window – why, just
pull yourself together and remember . . . that after all, there are
such things!

CHAPTER FOUR

BELA AND BORIS: A DEADLY DUO!

The love-bite, it is the beginning. In the end, you too, Boris, will become a vampire! You will live 500 years. You will sleep in moldy graves at night, and make fiendish love to beauties by day. You will see generations live and die. You will see a girl baby born to some woman, and wait a mere sixteen to eighteen years for her to grow up, so that you can sink fangs into a soft white neck and drink a scarlet stream. You will be irresistible, for you will have in your powerful body the very heat of hell, the virility of Satan!

Bela Lugosi to Boris Karloff

(What follows are the facts regarding the cinematic teaming of Bela Lugosi and Boris Karloff, including what has become known as the infamous Bela and Boris feud. Unlike 1994's film, *Ed Wood*, this chapter presents both sides of the story. As you will discover, in Hollywood, fiction is not just stranger than truth – it is the blood which runs the film industry.)

Because of the financial and artistic success of *Dracula*, Bela Lugosi had attained the horror moniker of "the new Lon Chaney."

And, because of Bela's new box office attraction status, Carl Laemmle ordered a new work of horror to be written for Bela: a screen adaptation of Mary Wollstonecraft Shelley's 1831 novel of human experimentation – *Frankenstein*.

To movie aficionados and horror film lovers world wide, it has always been reported that Bela Lugosi turned down the role of Frankenstein's Monster (remember that Frankenstein was the doctor – the Monster was never given a name). The fact is, Bela never turned the role down; he was fired.

When Robert Florey, who was originally slated to direct *Frankenstein*, was first given the script, he read it over and immediately called Bela Lugosi (who was working on another film). Florey told Bela about the script and that he wanted him for the film's lead, the title role of Doctor Frankenstein, instead of the monster. Bela was pleased to learn that he was chosen to play the part of the doctor since he felt it would give him a chance to step out of his "monster" role of *Dracula*, and into the Hollywood role of a "leading man."

When the Hollywood trade papers heard the news that Bela intended to portray the doctor who created a man from the used body parts of murderers (corpses), the reactions were mixed. Some columnists wondered how audiences would react to Bela in a role where menace would take a backseat to emotion (Doctor Frankenstein is a highly emotional role). Other columnists assumed that, because Bela had only portrayed "bad guys," he probably couldn't handle the role which would have him wearing a white coat instead of donning a black cape. Still, others simply noted that Bela was headed into a starring role of another horror film written from a book published a century earlier. What none of these columnists understood was that Bela Lugosi was first and foremost an actor, and that actors play roles – good guys and bad guys, winners and losers. This was something the Hollywood scribes didn't understand then (not much has changed to this day).

Once Robert Florey had the script for *Frankenstein*, he immediately began to rework the storyline and modify some of the characterizations. Because he had picked Bela Lugosi to portray Doctor Frankenstein, Florey decided to make the doctor into a stereotypic mad scientist. Florey also wanted to make the film the ultimate horror movie. Because of this goal, the Florey version of *Frankenstein* was to include several scenes not found in the book.

One wild episode involves two peasants. Johann and Gretel are preparing to make love while Frankenstein's monster plays "Peeping Tom" at the cottage window. Then Johann teasingly plays with Gretel's chemise; then, he flings the chemise toward the camera, and it finally drapes rakishly over the foot of the bed. The excited monster breaks into the cottage, "eyes gleaming beastially," throws Johann into a corner, and attacks Gretel. The episode ends with a "close shot of the peasants' children -- trembling with fright, wide-eyed, listening to the commotion-- too terrified to utter a sound."

In another episode, a village puppet show with marionettes, ala Punch and Judy, honors the wedding guests as part of the festivities. Suddenly, a puppet of the devil appears and the Punch puppet squeals and beats him with his club.

In addition to the puppet-show episode, Florey's *Frankenstein* also contains an epilogue in the village church. After a chase scene, which culminates at the windmill with the deaths of Henry and the monster, Baron Frankenstein and Victor meet Elizabeth in the church, standing by a pillar, as the morning sun breaks over them. In the background, the broken figure of the old Baron kneels before the shadowy alter. The camera moves back with increasing speed as the church doors close slowly.

What is perhaps most surprising about Florey's original script, however, is the personalities of the protagonists. Frankenstein is simply a smug, bullying, mad doctor with little personality and no sympathy for his creation. The first time we see the monster and monster-maker together, after the laboratory creation sequence, Frankenstein is torturing his creature with a whip and hot poker. The monster is simply a howling, hellish demon, devoid of the profound sympathy that later secured a spot for Karloff's monster in movie mythology.

Robert Florey never had a chance to see his ideas implemented. Before the script ever made it to the Universal moguls, Florey was relieved of his duties as director (a studio's polite way of saying, "you're fired"). When Florey was released from the film, Bela lost his chance to play Doctor Frankenstein, although he was not yet aware of this.

With Robert Florey no longer involved in the filming of *Frankenstein*, the film took on a whole new artistic approach. The man now responsible for directing the film was James Whale. It is the result of his input that we see today when we watch the film at theater revivals or on home video.

James Whale (1889-1957) was not like anyone else in the cinema. Whale's background and career were so eccentric that it is difficult to find anyone comparable – least of all Tod Browning. Browning made *Dracula* the same year that Whale made *Frankenstein*; the two directors are often compared. Whale was a newcomer to Hollywood and the cinema. He had previously worked successfully in his native Britain as a man of the theater – actor, designer, and, ultimately, as a director. It was his most famous and successful stage production of R. C. Sheriff's war play, *Journey's End*, in 1928, that had brought him to America, first to stage the play in New York, then to film it in Hollywood. In his first film, Whale works through the heavily theatrical, over-emphatic style in the early scenes. He then moves toward the ease and fluency of later styles, reaching a point where the stage play takes on a powerful cinematic life of its own.

James Whale gave the following interview to *The New York Times*:

> I chose *Frankenstein* out of about 30 available stories because it was the strongest meat and gave me a chance to dabble in the macabre. I thought it would be an amusing thing to try and make what everybody knows to be a physical impossibility into the almost believable for 60 minutes. A director must be pretty bad if he can't get a thrill out of a war, murder, robbery. *Frankenstein* was a sensational picture. It offered fine pictorial possibilities, had two grand characterizations – and that is part of the fun of making pictures.

It was Whale's rewriting of the script that gave the monster its human qualities. Whale created the scene where the monster throws the little girl (Maria) into the lake and then, after realizing what he has just done, shows remorse and sobs. This scene was edited out of the original print of the film by Universal Studio's censors but was later put back into the film or video.

The replacement of Robert Florey with James Whale and the changes in the *Frankenstein* script were not the only changes to this classic film, the roundabout sequel to *Dracula* and the cinema's second sound-horror film. One major change concerned Bela Lugosi. Carl Laemmle, the film's producer, no longer wanted Bela to portray Doctor Frankenstein. Instead, he wanted to cast the tall Hungarian actor as the monster. Bela did not become aware of this change until he saw the final draft of the script. To say he was displeased would be a gross understatement.

During this time, while all of these changes were going on with *Fran-*

Figure 5 – Boris Karloff in full make-up as Frankenstein, a role which was originally to go to Bela. Because of the critical praise Boris received from this portrayal, Bela succumbed to the ever-present Hollywood curse of . . . jealousy; Bela hated Boris professionally and personally. (Copyright © 1931 by Universal Studios, Inc. Courtesy of MCA Publishing Rights, a Division of MCA Inc. All Rights Reserved)

kenstein, Bela was still promoting *Dracula.* In an interview with Los Angles radio station KFI, Bela gave the following promotional speech (shortly after giving this speech, Bela learned that he was slated to play Frankenstein's monster):

> I read the book *Dracula,* written by Bram Stoker, 18 years ago, and I have always dreamed of creating and playing this part of Dracula. Finally the opportunity came. I have played Dracula over one thousand times on the stage and people often ask me if I still retain my interest in the character. I do – intensely. Because many people regard the story of Dracula as a glorified superstition, the actor who plays the role is constantly engaged in a battle with the audience, in a sense, since he is constantly striving to make the character so real that the audience will believe in it. Now that I have appeared in the screen version of the story which Universal has just completed, I am, of course, not under the daily strain in the depiction of the character. My work in this direction was finished with the completion of the picture, but while it was being made, I was working more intensely to this point than I ever did on the stage. Although *Dracula* is a fanciful tale of a fictional character, it is actually a story which has many essential elements of truth. I was born and reared almost in the exact location of the story; and, I came to know what is looked upon as a superstition of ignorant people is really based on facts which are literally hell-raising in their strangeness – but which are true. Many people will leave the theater with a sniff at the fantastic character of the story, but many others who think just as deeply will gain insight into one of the most remarkable facts of human existence. *Dracula* is a story which has always had a powerful effect on the emotion of an audience and I think that the picture will be no less effective than the stage play. In fact, the motion picture should prove even more remarkable in this direction since things which could be talked on the stage can be shown on the screen in all their uncanny details.

After giving this speech and seeing the new (and final) draft of the screenplay of *Frankenstein,* which had him portraying the monster, Bela flew into a rage which was far more horrifying than any "creature" that he ever played on the silver screen. It was not necessarily the monster role which sent Bela over the edge; it was because the monster had no speaking lines. Bela screamed in broken English, "The Monster could be played by any half-wit extra who knows how to grunt! Without any dialogue and all that makeup, what do they need an actor for?" Without saying another word on the subject, Bela threw the script to the ground, lit a cigar, and marched out of the radio station.

Because he was still relatively new to the Hollywood system, Bela did not realize that he had no choice in the matter because of the way that film contracts were constructed. He was under contract to Universal Pictures for two films, the first was *Dracula* – the second was *Frankenstein*.

Once Bela became aware that he was legally bound to the film, he submitted to the role – albeit briefly.

After a close reading of the "new" *Frankenstein* script and taking notes on the physical description of the monster, Bela came up with his own makeup. He devised what he thought the monster should look like. What Bela had in mind was nothing like what Universal wanted. Bela thought that the monster should look like a cross between the Wolf Man and the Keeper of Men (the Keeper being a character of H. G. Wells in *The Island of Doctor Moreau*, later made into *The Lost Island* starring Charles Laughton and Bela Lugosi). When everyone saw what Bela looked like in his original makeup, they did not shudder because of fright, they laughed uncontrollably. One Hollywood trade paper reported on Bela's costuming:

> Bela Lugosi, in the starring role, will be built up with makeup and padding to resemble an 8-foot superman, Mary Shelley, wife of poet Percy Shelley, wrote in 1816. When Lugosi is made up, only his chin and eyes will be visible, greasepaint and putty completely hiding the rest of his face. Shoes to which nearly 12 inches have been added will complete the illusion.

It was at this point that Carl Laemmle ordered Bela to the quarters of master makeup artist Jack Pierce. Pierce had created the Wolf Man, the Mummy, and other Hollywood film creatures.

Under the skilled hands of Pierce, Bela underwent four hours of makeup work. This included having his entire face puttied and painted and the addition of over 50 pounds of dead weight put upon his body to give him the presence of a creature who found the simple act of movement a major physical challenge.

Though it has always been reported that Bela fought with Jack Pierce during the whole time his makeup was being applied and that Pierce went to Carl Laemmle to claim that he would not work another minute on Bela, which resulted in the release of Bela from the film. This is not true. The reason Bela was released from *Frankenstein* was because of the wounds he had received in the war. He could not move with the costume's added weight and he was not physically able to perform most of the movements that were required of the monster in the film. Contrary to popular belief, this did not displease Carl Laemmle. He was completely understanding; and, instead of releasing Bela from his contract, he offered him a starring role in another horror film, *Murders in the Rue Morgue*.

Bela did complete a 20-minute-screen test as the monster in his full makeup. Paul Ivano, who was a member of the technical team, recalled Bela's screen test in a 1976 interview:

> You know, Universal was running on a shoestring in those days and they didn't allow me time to properly plan a lighting layout. With a few assistants, we rushed onto the old *Dracula* sets and found that the only place we could properly light the scenes was from above, due to the Gothic nature of the staircase. We placed a few lights behind the pillars. But we still had the shadows of the scaffolding criss-crossing the actors. Also, with the time so limited, we had no time to build any tracks for the camera dollies and so the old Mitchell camera was set stationary behind the operating table with Bela lying on it. Behind was the old staircase from *Dracula*. We followed the extra, who portrayed Dr. Frankenstein, and David Frye down the steps and stopped with the action taking place behind the monster. Using a focal plain shutter we kept focus; however what we thought would be a problem with the lighting turned out to our advantage for it gave the scene a very artistic and yet nightmarish effect. Robert Florey loved this for he was very adept in the Germanic style of cinematography – like the *Cabinet of Dr. Caligari*. Even his own experimental films had the same atmosphere: surrealistic.
>
> Another reason for the stationary camera was the early sound hot boxes they had to use. We could move around at will during

the silent days, but now there was the sound records to consider. To add insult to injury, Bela, who hated makeup to begin with, was to lie on the table for the total test, half covered by a sheet and after a few bits of special effects – for we didn't have the elaborate electrical machines of Kenny Strickfaden to enhance the shoot and only used lighting effects and shadows to give us the bizarre angles and eerie effects – all Bela did was open his eyes, look to the camera and move a few fingers on one hand.

The test came out so beautiful, from the artistic and photographic point of view, that all the directors on the lot wanted to make the film. Who would have thought that after all the films that Robert and I have done that this rushed, unused footage would be the one that people today are most interested.

This screen-test film has since been destroyed by time because the film used was not chemically treated to protect it from oxidation – not uncommon for the films of this era.

When it was finally determined that Bela Lugosi would not be portraying the monster in *Frankenstein*, Carl Laemmle and the Universal moguls devised a list of seven actors to be considered for the role. Of the seven names listed, only one was well known: Claude Raines. All of these actors turned down the role and all, with the exception of Raines, were released from Universal. Raines later went on to star in another Universal horror film classic: *The Invisible Man*.

It is rather obvious now, the man chosen to play Frankenstein's monster was a relative newcomer to Hollywood, Boris Karloff.

There are many stories concerning the way that Boris Karloff garnered the role which made him a legend of the horror cinema. The true story is not as Hollywood-like as some may want to believe or as other writers have noted. In Karloff's own words, this is how he was discovered.

James Whale, the director, was lunching at a nearby table. Suddenly he caught my eye and beckoned me over. I leapt – he was the most important director on the lot. He asked me to sit down. I did, holding my breath, and then he said, "Your face has startling possibilities." I cast my eyes down modestly and then he said, "I'd like to test you for the monster in Frankenstein." It was shattering – for the first time in my life I had been gainfully employed long enough to buy myself some new clothes and spruce up a bit – actually, I rather fancied myself. Now, to hide all this new-found under monster make-up? I said I'd be delighted.

As history has proven, it was the acting ability of Boris Karloff which gave Frankenstein's monster its life, not just that infamous bolt of lightening which found its fiery way into the good doctor's laboratory roof. It was after the film was shot that Carl Laemmle, having witnessed Karloff's incredible performance, had Edward Van Sloan (Doctor Van Helsing in *Dracula*) record a prologue for the film in the guise of a warning. It read:

How do you do? Mr. Carl Laemmle feels it would be a little unkind to present this picture without just a word of friendly warning. We are about to unfold the story of Frankenstein, a man of science, who sought to create a man after his own image – without reckoning upon God.

It is one of the strangest tales ever told. It deals with the two great mysteries of creation – life and death.

I think it will thrill you. It may shock you. It might even . . . horrify you! So if any of you feel you do not care to subject your nerves to such a strain, now is your chance to . . . well, we've warned you!

William Henry Pratt, who later became known as Boris Karloff, was born on November 23, 1887, in Dulwich, England. He was the son of a civil servant in the British foreign service, and the youngest of eight children and should have been destined for a diplomatic career. But in 1909, he emigrated to Canada, where he found employment as a farmhand. He was attracted to the stage and joined one touring company after another. For a decade, he played supporting parts in plays all over Canada and the United States. Then in 1916, during a brief stay in Los Angeles, he made his screen debut as an extra in *The Dumb Girl of Portici*, starring Anna Pavlovs. When his job ended three years later, he returned to Hollywood and began appearing regularly in films, in extra and bit parts. Because he was unable to support himself as an actor, he alternated between acting and truck driving. He did this until the mid-20's, when his screen roles became more substantial. He was typically cast as a stock villain and failed to gain much recognition through the rest of the silent era, although he appeared in no less than 50 silent films.

Despite a pronounced lisp, Karloff's stage-trained voice became an asset during the film industries transition to sound. He scored his first success in *The Criminal Code* (1931), in which he repeated the previous stage role. The real turning point in his career came later that year, when he was cast in the role of the monster in *Frankenstein*. Even the heavy makeup applied by Jack Pierce to Karloff's face could not hide the nuances of his performance. The film was a great success and assured Karloff a permanent niche in horror. During the Universal horror cycle of the early 30's and in so many such films that followed, he and his now frequent screen partner, Lugosi, formed the most formidable duo of the macabre in film history. Karloff also played many supporting parts out of the usual horror characterization. He notably played the part of a religious fanatic in John Ford's film, *The Lost Patrol* (1934). But, he remained identified in the public mind exclusively from his roles as a scarred, tortured, humanely vulnerable monster or a deranged scientist.

In contrast to the characters he portrayed, Karloff was known offstage as a mild mannered, amiable gentleman who performed many acts of charity for needy children. He narrated a Mother Goose story record and played the kind Colonel March of Scotland Yard on television. He also hosted and occasionally starred in a suspense television series called *Thriller*. Throughout his busy screen career (140 films), Karloff continued to return to the stage. He scored a great success in 1941 as Jonathan Brewster in the Broadway production of *Arsenic and Old Lace* and another in 1950 as Captain Hook in *Peter Pan*. He gave one of his best performances in one of his last screen roles, virtually playing himself, an aging star of horror movies, in Peter Bogdanovich's *Targets* (1968). Boris Karloff died in 1969; but, his legend will live on forever.

Shortly after his departure from the *Frankenstein* film, Bela shared his opinions about playing in horror films with the press, and described what he thought of the role of Frankenstein's monster. He believed that an actor can't make people believe in his character if he plays a horror part with his tongue in his cheek. The screen magnifies everything, even the way someone is thinking. If an actor is not serious, people will sense it. No matter how hokum or highly melodramatic the horror part may be, he must believe in it while he is playing it.

In the history of the cinema, there has never been a greater competition among thespians than the one between Bela Lugosi and Boris Karloff.

Or, at least that is what Hollywood lore would lead us to believe. Though Bela would never admit it, this competition was all his own doing. Because Bela did not take the role of Frankenstein's monster, it opened the theater door for Boris Karloff. Karloff didn't just walk through this door – he knocked the door right off its hinges! Within a couple of years of Karloff's legendary portrayal, he was Bela's main rival for the title of King of Horror. But, Karloff never could match Bela as Master of the Macabre. Because of these roles, Bela had garnered the title of "the evilest man in Hollywood."

As the rivalry between the two movie monsters grew, Universal Pictures made the wise business decision to combine the two men in films. This not only fueled the Hollywood speculation about the feuding and rivalry, it also caused theater box office registers to ring up record-breaking receipts. As with most Hollywood myths, fiction outweighs the facts. Although the Bela and Boris rivalry was indeed intense, it was also more artistic than personal – at least on the side of Boris Karloff. Karloff felt no ill will against Bela.

> "Poor old Bela," Karloff once commented, "it was a strange thing. He was really a shy, sensitive, talented man who had a fine career on the classical stage in Europe. But he made a fatal mistake. He never took the trouble to learn our language. He had a real problem with his speech and difficulty interpreting lines. This kept him from going farther than he could have and contributed to him being typecast."

Bela's feelings toward Karloff were not so kind. Bela detested Karloff. He blamed Karloff for his artistic inactivity during the 40's, his lack of top billing (Karloff was always billed above Bela in film credits, film publicity and on theater marquees), and his lack of respect within the film community. All who knew Bela, on a personal-relationship level, and there were not many, expected this attitude toward Karloff. Bela had only himself to blame for his problems. After giving up the role of *Frankenstein*, he surrounded himself with business associates and agents who could best described as losers. He regretted giving up this role his entire life (though he did portray the monster years later in *Ghost of Frankenstein*). It seemed Bela could not say no to any film offered to him, regardless of the script or the money. With Boris Karloff, everything was exactly opposite – he had a decent agent, smart business associates, and, for the most part, excellent perceptions of which films and roles to accept and which to decline.

In 1934, Universal Pictures finally decided to team the two movie monsters together in the film *The Black Cat,* supposedly adapted from Edgar Allan Poe's story.

> A revengeful doctor seeks out the Austrian architect and devil-worshiper who betrayed his country in World War I. Absurd and dense farrago set in a modernistic but crumbling castle which is eventually blown to bits just as its owner is skinned alive. Mostly rather dull despite the extraordinary plot, but the thing has moments of style, a delightful devil worship sequence (especially for audiences with a rudimentary knowledge of Latin) and nothing at all to do with the title or Edgar Allan Poe.
>
> Leslie Halliwell, *Halliwell's Film Guide*

The Black Cat, an unsung classic of the horror cinema, has an eerie story line, which somewhat parallels Bela's early life in Hungary. The film's fictional locale is Hungary. Bela plays a World War I veteran who flirted with death in the war and has since been given a chance for revenge toward his enemy (though in Bela's real life, his revenge was more mental than physical). This is Bela's only American-produced film in which he speaks his native language, though it is only in one scene.

Because this film was produced in 1934, a few modern touches almost slap the viewer in the face. There are digital clocks throughout the most modern of houses (modern even by today's standards), and everything is run via remote control, including a stereo sound system and the art-deco lighting. This area alone causes the film to come across as more science fiction than horror. In reference to the ultra modern house where Karloff's character lives (which is constructed over a cemetery containing the bodies of the war dead), Bela said, "A masterpiece of construction built upon a masterpiece of destruction." By the time the film ends, this statement is not only prophetic, but a very brilliant deduction.

There are some oddities in this film: Boris Karloff laughs (frightening by itself) and Bela cries (horror of horrors). At one point, Bela quips to Boris, "Are we men or are we children?" Considering the way Bela acted toward Boris in later years; it should have been Boris asking this question of Bela.

Unlike the other horror films produced by Universal, *The Black Cat* does not possess any of the stereotypical notions audiences are accustomed to and associate with the horror cinema, even in the late 1990's. Instead of screams in the night and the rolling bass of thunder, we hear the melodies of Liszt's *Rano Sonata in B*, Schumann's *Quintet in E flat Major* and some Tschaikovsky. Instead of presenting the evil villain as a character we immediately hate, Karloff is given a magnetic personality with a few likable qualities. The "good guy," Lugosi, is somewhat callous. And, instead of the Hollywood "good guy" halo, he has more of a just-sprouting set of devilish horns. (It is also one of his few films where Bela is not contrived to be evil.)

Of course, when audiences view *The Black Cat*, all eyes focus on the scene where Bela and Boris cavort together. In Danny Peary's outstanding reference book *Cult Movies #3*, he gives a very insightful observation on watching the two horror legends together:

> Karloff's deadpan, tongue-in-cheek performance is perfectly balanced by Lugosi, whose early dignified manner soon gives way to his singular brand of histrionics (an artificial display of emotion). It's a joy listening to the conversations between two actors, with such different accents and speech patterns.

This first teaming of Bela and Boris was eagerly anticipated by both film fans and Universal Pictures (fans for the entertainment value and Universal for the monetary value). But, Edgar Ulmer, the director of *The Black Cat*, soon learned that working with Bela Lugosi was not one of the greatest thrills a director could enjoy on the set (especially if Boris Karloff was an cast member of equal status). Ulmer once recalled:

> Karloff was very charming. My biggest part was to keep him in the part, because he laughed at himself. Not the Hungarian, of course. You had to cut away from Lugosi continuously, to cut him down to size. One of the nicest scenes I had with Karloff was when he was lying in bed on the set next to the Lugosi's character's daughter. A young couple rings the door bell and Karloff gets out of bed to answer the door. This is the first time you see him in costume. I explained the scene to him and he said, "Aren't you ashamed to do anything like that – that has nothing to do with acting?" So I told him to be nice and do it,

and he never took himself seriously – he got into bed, we got ready to shoot and he got up, he turned to the camera, after he put his shoes on, and said 'Boo!' Every time I had him come in by a door, he would open the door and say, "Here comes the heavy . . ." He was a very, very lovely man.

Ulmer's remarks point out yet another reason for the legendary Bela vs. Boris rivalry. Boris never really took himself seriously and Bela never took himself lightly – both of these facts are magnified in the deadly duo's films, where Boris always underacts and Bela always overacts. In Bela's defense, however, taking himself seriously was bred into him, because of his old-country European upbringing and his training on the European stage.

This film is as loosely based on Poe as a screen adaptation could possibly be and still have the author's name on the title. Because of this, the storyline is not what lures the audience to the film (the obvious lure is Bela and Boris). It is the ultramodern house built atop a graveyard, an idea solely from the mind of Edgar Ulmer. In a conversation with film director Peter Bogdanovich, Ulmer described how he got the idea for this location.

That came out many years before I met Gustav Meyrinck, the man who wrote *Golem* as a novel. Meyrinck was one of these strange Prague Jews, like Kafka, who was very much tied in the mystic Talmudic background. We had a lot of discussions, and Meyrinck at that time was contemplating a play based upon Doumont, which was a French fortress the German's shelled to pieces during the first World War. There were some survivors who didn't come out for years. And the commander was a strange Euripides figure who went crazy three years later when he was brought back to Paris, because he had walked on that mountain of bodies. And I thought it was a great subject that was quite important. And that feeling was in the air in the twenties. I wanted to write a novel really, because I did not believe the literature after the war and during the war, on both sides. In Germany and in England, war was very much the heroic thing... I couldn't believe that. Therefore, I took two men who knew each other and who fought their private war during the time that capitalism flourished. I thought it was quite a story stylistically. I had a wonderful cameraman [John Mescall], and producer [Carl Laemmle] let me do the set and everything at the same time. It was very much out of my Bauhaus period.

The two most memorable scenes from this classic are the infamous chess game where the winner gets the heroine (she dies if Boris wins and she is saved if Bela wins) and the scene where Bela skins Boris alive.

During the chess game, both actors play for all they are worth. The studio must have loved this as much as the audience, because, after the scene was shot, the studio filmed Bela and Boris over the chess board as themselves. They did this to publicize not just *The Black Cat*, but also *Dracula* and *Frankenstein* (the studio was getting ready to re-release both films as part of what became a record-breaking double feature). The lines recited by both men were ad-libbed and, as usual, Bela made every attempt to upstage Karloff. He said:

> Ah Boris, to win a woman, take her with you to see *Dracula*, the movie. As she sees me, the bat-like vampire, swoop through an open casement into some girl's boudoir, there to sink teeth into neck and drink blood, she will thrill through every nerve and fiber. That is your cue to draw her close, Boris. When she is limp as a rag, take her where you will, do with her what you will. Ah, especially, Boris, bite her on the neck!
>
> The love-bite, it is the beginning. In the end, you too, Boris, will become a vampire! You will live five hundred years. You will sleep in moldy graves at night, and make fiendish love to beauties by day. You will see generations live and die. You will see a girl baby born to some woman, and wait a mere sixteen to eighteen years for her to grow up, so that you can sink fangs into a soft white neck and drink a scarlet stream. You will be irresistible for you will have in your powerful body the very heat of hell, the virility of Satan.

The scene where Bela skinned Boris alive was so real, even though it is filmed in silhouette and shadows, that the British Film Board banned the film. The banning of *The Black Cat*, and also of *The Raven*, resulted in the across-the-boarder ban on horror films throughout the British Isles – a ban which was crucial in the ultimate demise of Bela Lugosi's career.

When asked to sum up *The Black Cat*, film historian and critic Carlos Clarens, gave this one line critique: "A contrived catalogue of Satanism, necrophilia, sadism, and murder." This may explain why the movie is just as popular today on home video as it was back in the 30's on the silver screen.

To take full advantage of the success of *The Black Cat* and the popularity of Bela and Boris together (in both the film credits and promotions, Boris was simply listed as Karloff, his first name never being used), Universal rushed the two back to the studio to make *The Raven*.

Reviews were mixed, but generally positive. Some praised Universal Studios for maintaining the shock value its horror films have been known for in the making of *The Raven*. Another said *The Raven* had nothing to do with Poe's poem but it was certainly the inspiration for the torture implemented by the mad Bela Lugosi on Boris Karloff. Then, another review said *The Raven* was the worst horror film of the season, a fatal mistake.

Like *The Black Cat*, *The Raven* had Edgar Allan Poe's name all over the publicity material, though it does not even come close to Poe's classic poem. The only relation to Poe offered by this film is that Bela's character, Doctor Vollin, is enamored by Poe and cites the master storyteller often.

The Raven is actually a look at the Bela vs. Boris controversy. During the time of the filming, Bela began to dislike Boris, both personally and professionally. Bela realized Boris was his main rival as the King of Horror; and, as it is evident by viewing this film, Bela revelled in his character because he was able to take control of Karloff and treat him as he wished to do in real life. The scenes where Bela fictionally tortures Karloff represent some of the best acting that Bela has ever done.

"There were times during the filming when I had to tell Bela to calm down," admitted Louis Friedlander, the films director. "Bela was an incredible talent and I was fully aware of his training which is why I thought he was so intense in his scene with Karloff. Then someone told me that Bela detested Boris. 'A-ha,' I thought, and I took full advantage of these feelings and I think the dislike is what actually made the film the classic it has become."

Because the film relied on the intensity between Bela and Boris, filming proceeded better than expected and it came in under budget. The film took 16 days to shoot and cost only $150,000 to produce. Of course, it did help the budget when Universal decided to use the *Bride of Frankenstein* set for filming *The Raven*.

In later years, Bela often said his portrayal of Doctor Vollin in *The Raven* was one of his favorite roles. Like the character of Doctor Vollin, Bela was a big fan of Edgar Allan Poe and one of the most literate actors of his time. Bela's love of Poe is evident when he delivers the following address in *The Raven*, which sets the tone of the film:

> Poe was a great genius. Like all great geniuses, there was in him the insistent will to do something big, great, constructive in the world. He had the brain to do it. But he fell in love. Her name was Lenore.
>
> Something happened. Someone took her away from him. When a man of genius is denied of his great love, he goes mad. His brain, instead of being clear to do his work, is tortured, so he begins to think of torture. Torture for those who have tortured him. My interest in Poe, the way I speak about torture and death, you people being laymen perhaps do not understand. As a doctor, a surgeon, I look upon these things differently. A doctor is fascinated by death – and pain. And how much pain a man can endure.

When *The Raven* finally made it across the Atlantic to the movie theaters of Great Britain, *The Black Cat* was still fresh in the minds of the British Board of Censors. After viewing *The Raven*, they issued a warning to all American film studios that this type of horror film was "unfortunate and undesirable" and would not be allowed in Great Britain. This ban took the entire American film community by surprise – and the shock waves reverberated all the way to the bank.

The American motion picture industry garnered a great deal of money from the film audiences of Great Britain (just like today). The 30's was the decade of horror cinema; but, American studios had to abide by the British Board of Censors ruling – or get around it in a roundabout way. Instead of sending the original versions of horror films to Great Britain, the studios shipped edited versions – some were edited to the point that the story made very little sense. The British ban damaged the American film industry and had a devastating effect on actors and actresses who played in the horror cinema – including Bela Lugosi.

Bela tried to keep a stiff upper lip when he heard about the British ban on American horror films. Although he defended the horror genre, he begged for non-horror roles, evidenced by his following statement:

> The popularity of horror pictures in understandable. The screen is the ideal medium for the presentation of gruesome tales, and they have almost universal appeal. Although, I am afraid I'm typed by now, I'd like to quit the supernatural roles every third time and play just an interesting, down-to-earth person. One of these days, I may get my wish! Meanwhile, I'll take any story if it's good.

And for the most part, Bela did take any story – whether it was good or not.

The Invisible Ray was blood-curdling, typical of Universal horror pictures. Although, the scenes of Africa aren't realistic, the part about the radium eating up Janus Rukh (Karloff) is a dynamic ending. Bela Lugosi as Dr. Felix Benet impressed audiences as the sympathetic scientist.

The Invisible Ray was one of those rare films of the 30's (1936) which blended horror and science fiction successfully.

Carl Laemmle, the producer of *The Invisible Ray*, knew the names Karloff and Lugosi would bring people into the theaters. But, he wanted more – he wanted the audience to believe the storyline was more science-fact than science-fiction. Toward that end, Laemmle followed the opening credits with this statement:

> Every scientific fact accepted today once burned as a fantastic fire in the mind of someone called mad.
>
> Who are we on this youngest and smallest of planets to say that the *Invisible Ray* is impossible to science?
>
> That which you are about to see is a theory whispered in the cloisters of science. Tomorrow these theories may startle the universe as fact.

An interesting aspect of this film, the deadly duo's third team up, is the way Bela delivered his lines to Boris' character, keeping alive the Bela vs. Boris conflict. With every line, Bela spoke down to Boris in a manner not written into the script. Lambert Hillyer, director of *The Invisible Ray* said:

At first I thought the tone in Bela's voice was just part of his accent and natural delivery, but when I asked him to change his delivery, his response to me was curt. "I can't change the way I feel. My character is the better person and I must show this!" When I explained to Bela that he and Boris' character were equal (in the film's first half), he gave me that now famous Lugosi leered and uttered a few words in a language I didn't understand and which I suppose was Hungarian.

Those who have viewed *The Invisible Ray* are aware that Bela did not change his delivery of lines to Boris, which actually made the film better. It was because of this that the two became adversaries. With this in mind, one line in particular spoken by Boris is indeed interesting. Boris said to Bela: "You came to see me fail . . . . You and I have never seen eye to eye."

Another interesting point: *The Invisible Ray* was similar to the duo's first film *The Black Cat*; it was a prophetic film about high-technology. In *The Invisible Ray*, Boris used Radium X in his laser machine to cure his mother's blindness. Perhaps, Carl Laemmle's forward to this film was not as much publicity "hype" as was originally thought.

Three years after *The Invisible Ray*, Universal brought Bela and Boris together once again. This time, Boris revived his most famous character, Dracula, and Bela played a new character in *Son of Frankenstein* – a character that would rival Dracula as a horror legend.

Response to *Son of Frankenstein* from movie reviewers was mixed. It was called a masterpiece in production settings and special effects. It was said that the picture was well directed and the cast was appropriately chosen for a horror film skillfully done. Some felt Bela and Boris overacted in this film making it one of the silliest films ever produced. It was also written that the skillfully chosen actors throw themselves entirely into their roles in *Son of Frankenstein*.

Son of Frankenstein was made for purely economic reasons. In 1939, Universal Pictures had re-released *Dracula* and *Frankenstein* as a double-feature. They were so popular that during its theatrical run, the total gross receipts were more than both films had made during their original runs in theaters nationwide. It is ranked as one of the top five horror films of all-time, alongside of *Dracula, Frankenstein, Bride of Frankenstein, The Mummy*, and *The Phantom of the Opera* (the original silent version starring Lon Chaney Sr.).

Son of Frankenstein was the last time Boris Karloff was to play the monster. This was because he did not film well in Technicolor. When the film began in October of 1938, it had been written with color in mind. After the first few days of filming, Rowland V. Lee (the film's director) was not pleased with the way Boris' makeup showed up on film. Instead of the makeup filming as the focal point of the monster scenes, it was bleeding into the scenery. New shades of makeup were used in order to bring the monster out, but all failed. Throwing his hands into the air, Lee went to the film producer, Carl Laemmle, and stated that the film would have to be shot in black and white.

Rowland Lee recalled his meeting with Laemmle:

> Carl Laemmle threw a fit. He started screaming at me, mixing his native German with English. Universal had spent a great deal of money in the trade papers promoting that the film was going to be shot in color; that the world would finally get to see what the Monster looked like. "What am I going to do now," Laemmle asked me? "What am I going to do to get the interest in the film at fever pitch?" My response was simple. I told him to get Bela and make this another Boris and Bela film. Now, you must understand two things here. First, Carl Laemmle was good friends with Boris and did not like the things Bela had been saying about him around Hollywood. Second, at this time, Bela was on the skids as far as his career was concerned. Anyway, I talked Carl into letting me have Bela and in return I had to have Willis Cooper rewrite the script with me and together we created the role of Ygor.

What Rowland Lee failed to mention: To create the role of Ygor and bring Bela on board, Lee had to release Dwight Frye (Frye was the original assistant, humped back and all, to Colin Clive in *Frankenstein* and *The Bride of Frankenstein*).

Bela was extremely grateful to Rowland Lee for creating the role of Ygor for him because Bela was desperate for any film roles. This was caused by the British ban on American horror films; studios were making fewer horror films. And, because Bela had been typecast into the horror-film genre, he was not working much. Bela, delighted about Lee's decision to cast him in *Son of Frankenstein*, once noted:

> . . . for *Dracula* I used no heavy makeup but for *Son of*

Frankenstein – God he was cute! He was first a little part but every day the director makes him bigger and finally he is the biggest part in the picture.

Although Bela was grateful to Lee for creating the role of Ygor, he should also have been more grateful to another member of the cast who went to bat for him . . . Boris Karloff.

When it became obvious that Bela would be replacing Frye in *Son of Frankenstein*, Boris approached Lee about how the character of Ygor should be created to showcase all of Bela's talents. Boris did this for only one reason; he knew that Bela was having financial problems. If the film showcased Bela's theatrical range, more film executives would notice his skill as an artist. Whether or not Bela ever knew of Boris' involvement in this matter is not known.

Grateful for Lee's favor, Bela gave one of his most beloved performances. Never in the history of the horror cinema has a murderous, deformed creature evoked so much human emotion. Although Dracula is the role Bela is most noted for, it is his role as Ygor which finally got Bela the chance to show his true acting ability. And what did Bela receive for this role – a role and performance which stole the film? A resounding $500 a week!

Concerning Bela's portrayal of Ygor, Lee said:

> Bela was greatly underestimated by the studio. We gave him his sides as Ygor and let him work on the characterizations; the interpretation he gave us was imaginative, and totally unexpected. It wasn't Dracula at all, in fact, quite the opposite. He played Ygor as a rogue, but one that evoked sympathy. There was warmth in his voice and a twinkle in his eyes that made him almost lovable. When we finished shooting, there was no doubt in anyone's mind that he stole the show. Karloff's Monster was weak by comparison.

The most interesting aspect about *Son of Frankenstein* was its filming. The film had a budget of $300,000 and 27 days to complete production. Although that was not unusual for this era in Hollywood, the way the film was produced was.

Contrary to popular belief, *Son of Frankenstein* was filmed without a script. The director had a scenario for each segment of filming – he did not have any of the actors' lines. The lines were written and re-written just before filming each scene. This strange way of filming caused Josephine Hutchinson (who portrayed Mrs. Frankenstein) to comment: "Though the filmmaking was an interesting experience, the director was constantly having dialogue rewritten on the set. I had to constantly study new lines. I didn't care for it."

Son of Frankenstein was completed on time and only $117,000 over budget. However, to complete the film, edit it, preview it, and get it to the theaters on time, took a Herculean effort by Lee.

Filming ended on January 5. The picture was edited in a single day on January 6, previewed on January 7, and opened in theaters across the nation on January 10.

Two glaring mistakes are outstanding in *Son of Frankenstein*. First, although it is obvious that the film takes place in Germany, there is talk of a Scotland Yard investigation and a castle is mentioned as if it were located in the Carpathian Mountains (Great Britain and Hungarian locales). This occurred because the film was written on a daily basis and because of the war. Lee wanted all references to Germany omitted.

The second mistake involves Bela's character, Ygor. Supposedly he was the victim of an unsuccessful hanging which broke his neck. Sometimes his head cocks to one side, making it obvious that his neck was broken; and at other times, he moves his head around freely. In *Young Frankenstein*, Mel Brooks parodies this inconsistency by giving his Ygor (Marty Feldman) a hump which moves from his right shoulder to his left with each new scene.

The final film which starred Bela Lugosi and Boris Karloff was the 1945 version of Robert Louis Stevenson's *The Body Snatcher*. Although they were together in other films, they were not in the same scene.

Val Lewton's production of *The Body Snatcher* measured high in humane sincerity and devotion to good cinema; but, it was said to be more literary than melodramatic. Boris presented a spine-chilling characterization of the blackmailing, graver-robber. Bela portrayed the snooping houseman who provided corpses for the mad doctor's research.

Although *The Body Snatcher* is now remembered as the last film starring Bela Lugosi *and* Boris Karloff, it is actually much more; it is a classic of the horror cinema and represents Val Lewton's shining hour.

RKO producer Val Lewton's 1940's. fright-film series ranked as a type of Masterpiece Theater of horror movies. At a time when Hollywood's reigning horror studio, Universal, was relying on sickly crafted but increasingly formulated recycling of their once classic creatures (e.g. *Frankenstein Meets the Wolf Man*), and small outfits like Monogram and PRC were cranking out creepy quickies, Lewton navigated the horror genre in a new direction. Lewton rejected mad scientists and fright-masked monsters in favor of literate evocations of the silent and unseen. He often taped his own nightmares for inspiration.

Lewton (real name: Vladimir Leventon) was an experienced fiction writer and former editorial assistant to David O. Selznick. This 38-year-old Russian-born producer signed on to oversee RKO's newly formed horror unit in 1942. Lewton was to have complete creative control, as long as he agreed to work from the studio's sensationalistic, test-marketed titles (*Curse of the Cat People, I Walked With a Zombie*, etc.). He also had to agree to produce his "B" films for less than $150,000 each and to limit their length to 75 minutes. Lewton assembled a creative team of directors including Robert Wise, Mark Robson and Jaques Tourner, and scripter DeWitt Bodeen. With these men who shared his vision, Lewton produced a series of moody cult classics that, despite their deliberately misleading monikers, rethought and revitalized the horror genre.

Lewton left RKO in 1946 for a series of higher paying but unsuccessful production assignments at Paramount, Universal, and M-G-M. When he returned to RKO, he discovered that his power had been wrested away from him by former proteges Wise, Robson and Tourner. They hired Lewton as a story editor and then fired him. Lewton succumbed to a fatal heart attack in 1951 at the age of 46.

With the exception of 1943's *Ghost Ship* (which never made it past an initial release because of an unresolved plagiarism suit), Lewton and crew's entire eerie oeuvre is now available on video.

The Body Snatcher, may possibly be the best period piece in American cinematic history because the intricate sets resembled Edinburgh, Scotland, of the 1800's This includes all aspects of the medical world during this period as well. The scenes featuring Henry Daniell (the mad doctor) and his medical students were so authentic that the film has been reviewed and studied in various medical colleges for its authenticity in 19th century anatomy instructions. Although the scenes may be boring to some of the audience, the decision to include them was a stroke of genius by the film's writer, Carlos Keith. These scenes brought authenticity to the film. Carlos Keith was a pseudonym for Val Lewton.

In 1944, when *The Body Snatcher* was filmed (released in 1945),

Bela Lugosi was a drug addict and an alcoholic. He was well on his way to becoming a Hollywood has-been. His dislike for Karloff now teetered on the verge of utter hatred (all because of jealousy). But, when he was offered the small role as Henry Daniell's manservant, he had no other choice but to accept it.

Val Lewton commented about creating the characater of Ygor for Bela:

> As a matter of fact, it was really a manufactured role in order to work him into the film. The role was actually created for Lugosi and probably would not have existed in the screenplay if Lugosi had not been available or had not liked the part.

Bela's addiction to alcohol and drugs was not common knowledge at the time. This caused Lewton to be somewhat taken back by the way Bela acted during the filming of *The Body Snatcher*, Lewton recalled:

> Bela was not the quickest or sharpest of mind anymore. I got the impression that he might have been ill recently. Karloff was recovering from a back operation at the same time, so we had to handle both of them with kid gloves. Bela was most coopera-tive, and he obviously worked hard at preparing his part, but his memory failed him more than occasionally. Honestly, it was a bit of a chore with him. I knew he was working hard, and it embarrassed me to ask him for so many retakes, but everything worked out in the end. We were very pleased with the final product.

According to Hollywood lore and, most recently, Tim Burton (author of a biography about the legendary film-director Ed Wood), the so-called feud between Bela Lugosi and Boris Karloff was basically one-sided. Boris once said of his film rival:

> Bela was a fine actor and a fine man, but his main problem was that he never really caught on to the English language. If Bela would have had a command of the language, his roles would have been more versatile – he would have become the star he always thought he was.

Because Boris' statement is true, Bela's feelings toward Boris can be described in one word, jealousy. Bela was jealous of Boris because he often won feature roles from Bela. Bela was also jealous of Boris because he was popular, he was making money and because he was never really typecast in the horror genre and B-films. Bela also knew his reluctance to portray Frankenstein's monster created Boris Karloff, the screen actor. Bela was a proud man, so he would never admit to himself that he alone was to blame for what went before. Self-blame was a feeling Bela never would, or could, admit.

Up until the day Bela died, whenever the name Boris Karloff was mentioned, Bela would utter various profanities in Hungarian. And he always included, in English, "that son-of-a-bitch with a lisp."

Regardless of Bela's feelings toward Boris, these two Masters of Mayhem, were the horror genre's deadliest duo during Hollywood's Golden Era. The names Lugosi and Karloff, shining in neon on a theater marquee (always listed only by their last names), meant box-office cash registers would ring and seats would be filled.

Probably the greatest tribute ever paid to Bela Lugosi and Boris Karloff, who have caused more nightmares than the ever-present "monster-under-the-bed," is that they scared theater-goers out of their wits. And, they accomplished this without ever showing any graphic slicing, slashing or thrashing of human anatomy. They never once repulsed their audience with gallons of blood or handfuls of human entrails, flayed to and fro. Bela and Boris scared viewers with their craft – with their art – something which surely cannot be said of today's horror films or the actors who star in these films.

CHAPTER FIVE

MADNESS, MAYHEM, AND THE MACABRE

You can't make people believe in you if you play a horror part with your tongue in your cheek. The screen magnifies everything, even the way you are thinking. If you are not serious, people will sense it. No matter how hokum or highly melodramatic the horror part may be, you must believe in it while you are playing it.

Bela Lugosi

After Bela Lugosi's immense success in *Dracula*, he was in demand. Then when Universal Pictures realized the money *Dracula* was making, Carl Laemmle went to work to find another vehicle of horror, featuring Bela and capitalizing on both his name and persona. Laemmle chose Mary Shelley's *Frankenstein* and his choice of actors to portray, what would become, Hollywood's most famous monster was Bela Lugosi. As fate would have it, physical restrictions prohibited Bela from portraying the monster, which eventually became immortalized by Boris Karloff.

Laemmle did not want to lose the magic with which Bela captivated audiences or his box office attraction. So, he came up with another horror movie for Bela (Bela was under contract for two films). Since Bela could not portray Frankenstein's monster, Laemmle portrayed him as a more human monster, Doctor Mirakle, in a film loosely based on Edgar Allan Poe's story, *Murders in the Rue Morgue*.

"I knew exactly what I was doing when I had *Murders in the Rue Morgue* adapted for the screen and Lugosi," commented Carl Laemmle. "Just take a look at Mirakle – he is Dracula without the physical appetite for blood – but with the same appetite for death. Looking back, it was actually a blessing that Bela could not play the monster in *Frankenstein*, because if he had, *Murders in the Rue Morgue* would not have been made by Universal (which was the only major motion picture producing horror films at this time in Hollywood), Karloff would still be driving trucks and Bela would have missed out on one of his most menacing performances."

What Laemmle does not mention here is that he could adapt Poe's stories to films without paying a royalty to the author. Because Poe's works are considered "public domain," Laemmle, a real penny pincher, had a no-cost source of story lines. This was the case with most of the horror films that Universal adapted for the screen, which also explains why so many of Poe's stories were turned into films.

YOU THRILLED TO *DRACULA*!
YOU GASPED AT *FRANKENSTEIN*!
NOW COMES THE SUPER-SHOCKER OF THEM ALL!
MURDERS IN THE RUE MORGUE!

This was the theatrical trailer for *Murders in the Rue Morgue* and Universal Pictures – Laemmle in particular – took full advantage of its two-film predecessors by linking the names *Dracula* and *Frankenstein* with the film. Since the whole world was now agog over both of these films. Laemmle knew that the very same audiences would flock to the theaters to see *Murders in the Rue Morgue*.

Murders in the Rue Morgue was Universal's third horror film in a series of spine-tingling dramas. In turn-of-the-century Paris, Bela as Dr. Mirakle believes mating beautiful virgins with an ape named Erik would result in a perfect union between man and animal. Mirakle also secretly injects women with ape blood and then dumps the dead victims into the river. Erik kills people along the way and then stuffs them up chimneys. The story has little association with Edger Allan Poe, other than the story's title.

While doing some pre-publicity work for *Murders in the Rue Morgue*, Bela commented about accepting the role of Doctor Mirakle, a part created especially for him:

> Circumstances made me the theatrical personality I am, which many people believe is also a part of my personal life. My next picture, *Murders in the Rue Morgue*, will continue to establish me as a weird, gruesome creature. As for my own feeling on the subject, I have always felt I would rather play – say, Percy Marmont roles than Lon Chaney types of things.

Once the filming of *Murders in the Rue Morgue* began, Bela changed his mind about being "a weird, gruesome creature." After the filming, he was quoted as saying, "It was kind of nice to be in a horror film where I'm not some kind of monster. Here I am more human. Yes, human with a very dark side, but human nevertheless."

As much as Bela enjoyed working on *Murders in the Rue Morgue*, those he worked with did not consider the experience as enjoyable – at least not as far as working with Bela was concerned.

In the beginning, Sidney Fox was excited about working with Bela. Like every other woman, she found him sexy in an erotic way. But, once he came on the set, that all changed. When they weren't acting in a scene together, he would ignore her. And, when they were in a scene together, he'd try to outdo everyone. In the laboratory scene, it is said that he not only over-acted, but he was extremely rough with Fox.

Robert Florey, who created *Murders in the Rue Morgue* and directed its filming, also had some definite opinions about working with Bela. On the set, Bela was habitually silent, almost unwilling to converse. Between scenes, he slipped away to his dressing room. Because Florey was responsible for directing several actors, his conversation with Lugosi was limited to discussion about the scenes and how he should interpret them. Lugosi continually criticized the scenes.

Leon Ames, who was billed as Leon Waycoff in *Murders in the Rue Morgue*, also shared his memories of working with filmdom's Master of the Macabre:

Lugosi was a very quiet fellow and kept to himself during most of the shooting. I was very green in the acting profession then, and to me as a young man, Bela seemed very much the eerie Dracula character of his films.

The individual that Sidney Fox, Robert Florey, and Leon Ames came into contact with on the set was not only Bela Lugosi, the temperamental actor, but also Bela Lugosi, the egoist. Bela had an ego as big as the Hollywood Hills. Because of the success of *Dracula* and his other films, plus having *Murders in the Rue Morgue* adapted especially for him, his ego had ballooned over time. Bela was self-conscious about his poor use of the English language and he did not want to be laughed at – only to be laughed with.

In 1931, between *Dracula* and *Murders in the Rue Morgue*, Bela made the following films: *Women of All Nations, The Black Camel, Broadminded,* and *Fifty Million Frenchmen. Women of All Nations* was reminiscent of *The Cockneyed World,* a comedy by Mssrs. McLaglen and Lowe. In *The Black Camel,* Charlie Chan solves a 3-in-1 murder. Joe E. Brown, surrounded by a cast of pretty girls, gets the laughs in *Broadminded. Fifty Million Frenchmen* is a slapstick comedy with a light romance undertone.

None of these films could match Bela's portrayals of Count Dracula or Doctor Mirakle in artistic style or cinematic grace (not to mention audience appeal). But, *White Zombie,* his next film, did. Blood-curdling screams could be heard in theaters across America. *White Zombie* was the forefather to George Romero's cult classic, *The Night of the Living Dead,* and the precursor to all zombie (the walking dead) films.

Not only is the storyline in *White Zombie* especially interesting, so is the way it was constructed into film. It almost seems as if the Halperin Brothers (Victor, the director, and Edward, the producer of the film) wanted to make a silent film and added script only for the purpose of audience acceptance. This is by no means a criticism of this film. Quite to the contrary. Because of this mode of filming *White Zombie,* Bela's acting is more "scene-stealing" than usual. He delivers a truly evil performance – a nightmare come true.

Haitian zombies work a sugar mill for a white schemer. Genuinely eerie horror film with a slow, stagey, out-of-this world quality coupled with an interesting sense of composition.
Leslie Halliwell, *Halliwell's Film Guide*

While Victor and Edward Halperin prepared *White Zombie* for pro-duction (inspired by the play *Zombie*), they saw Bela's performance in the film version of *Dracula*. When they saw the magic Bela brought to his portrayal of the Count, they knew he was the man they needed to play the male lead in their film (Madge Bellamy was not only the female lead, she also received top billing). When *White Zombie* was ready to go into production, Bela had just completed *Murders in the Rue Morgue* and he was dead tired. At first he declined the role. But, after several meetings with the Halperin Brothers, Bela finally agreed. His motivation for finally accepting the role was not money (he was paid only $500 a week), it was the opportunity to co-direct the film (although uncredited). *White Zombie* is the only film in which Bela ever had a hand in behind-the-scenes activities.

Madge Bellamy was not impressed with Bela in his role as co-director:

> He was a total monster on that film and I mean a real monster – not his character. The few scenes they let him direct all he did was scream, rave and rant, and why, I still don't know, as these scenes had no dialogue and very little movement. They basically consisted of close-ups and distant shots of the castle interior. Let me put it this way, working with Bela Lugosi almost made all of us real zombies!

Dracula seems to have had a great influence on the Halperin Brothers because they continually used -- what was to become -- Bela's greatest screen asset, his eyes. Throughout this film, which is only a little over sixty minutes long, the close-ups of Bela's eyes are not only prominent, but almost constant. In almost every scene he is involved in, the camera almost always captures his incredible, naturally hypnotic eyes with all their evil glory.

By this time in his American career, Bela's personal life had become almost as mysterious as the fictional characters he portrayed. Hollywood tabloids looked for any gossip about him (his womanizing ways had subsided somewhat because he was working so many hours). So, when the studio did put out new press sheets on Bela, they were grabbed up with much gusto and glee by the entertainment media mavens.

One of the better press sheets, released in conjunction with *White Zombie,* read:

> There is something of a mysterious, hypnotic quality about

the man himself, particularly about his deep-set eyes, and the reason appears to be that he has probed life too deeply.

But probing life is just what he has devoted his thoughts to. Seldom has he dwelt upon this ambition, for he has few intimates and, with the exception of his studio visits, he is seen in public infrequently. He remains in his inaccessible retreat in the Hollywood mountains, and his constant companion is a half-wild malamute dog which howls at night . . .

The star unintentionally put all of his philosophy into one paragraph one day recently, when an interviewer managed to corner him at his home. Lugosi had been looking off into space towards the Pacific Ocean, when he suddenly swerved around and said:

"People – thousands of them – chained by monotony, afraid to think, clinging always to certainties and terrified by the unknown. They live like ants. I want to get away from people. I must get away somewhere where I can be free.

"And I can do it soon, too. Not many more years and I will have enough of this world's goods to pursue my own course and to pay for whatever research I desire to make. I'm going into the mountains completely away from people, to study.

"I have lived too completely, I think. I have known every human emotion. Fear, hate, hope, love, rage, despair, ambition – all are old acquaintances, but they have left nothing to offer me. Only study and reflection remain. I must know what I have learned. I must analyze all my theories and be alone to think."

Certainly, Bela Lugosi is an unhappy man. He is given to unaccountable moods, spells of silence during which he seems to be conversing with some unseen presence. Only one thing can be certain about him, and that is that any weird ingredients in his nature are bound to be marshaled upon the side of good rather than of evil . . . . For one of Bela Lugosi's fondest hopes is to exert some force in the agitation for a more Utopian existence.

This entire press sheet about Bela was a pack of lies – none of it true – but it did give the scribes who wrote for the tabloids loads of ammunition. This was always the studio's ultimate goal, where the press was concerned.

The quotes attributed to Bela in the press sheet were never said by him. Once again, the studio made up "strange" quotes just to get press attention for their star. The reason for this is really quite simple; if a star's name is in print and on the public's lips, people will relate to the star. This increases box office appeal, which results in more money for the studio (but seldom for the star). Roseanne and Madonna are two of today's celebrities subject to this kind of treatment.

During this same period of time, Bela did actually give an interview to Dorothy West. Judging from the following interview, she was not the Barbara Walters of her time. But, for the most part, Bela did tell the truth. And, for Bella, this was unusual. This is an example of a typical Hollywood "fluff" interview with major stars during Hollywood's heyday of the 1930's. From an historical perspective, this type of interview help create the myth that Hollywood is a type of Eden – a land where dreams came true. If Mike Wallace, Larry King or Phil Donahue had lived during this era of Hollywood, they would have revealed the truth, and scandals would have been common.

DOROTHY WEST: You're Hungarian, aren't you Mr. Lugosi?

BELA LUGOSI: Yes, I am. What I mean is I'm Hungarian by birth, I'm an American now [Bela became a citizen in late 1931].

DW: Why did you leave Hungary?

BL: Political reasons. After the war I participated in the revolution and later I found myself on the wrong side.

DW: Oh, that's very unfortunate. What are you studying now?

BL: I'm studying now American slang. I know how to say "okay," "cat's-whiskers" and "baloney" and "and how."

DW: But you did become a citizen, did you not?

BL: Oh, sometime ago and I'm very glad and happy about it. I can stay here for good. It's very nice to live in a country where people know how to mind their own business. And there's something else; it's wonderful how Americans display their sportsmanship.

DW: Mr. Lugosi, did you play any mystery parts in Europe?

BL: No, I didn't, by accident, I didn't.

DW: What types of roles did you play?

BL: Oh, different kinds of roles – character, dramatic, romantic – all kinds.

DW: Have you ever been interested in anything outside of your profession?

BL: Oh yes, very much. I like to model and sculpture.

DW: What was your first mystery play?

BL: It was *Dracula.*

DW: Did the role depress you?

BL: Very much. It haunted me. I often dreamed of the dead. In the morning when I woke up, I was tight, pressed. Did you see the play?

DW: No, I didn't. I'm awfully sorry. What kind of makeup did you use?

BL: It isn't so much the makeup, it's rather expression.

DW: I'm afraid I'll dream about this myself tonight. Were you satisfied with your work in the picture?

BL: No. When an actor gets satisfied with his work, he's done – he's through. You see, in the National Theater of Hungary in Budapest, all the great character parts are played by four or five different players. Each competes with the other, each plays the part in accordance with an old conception and the audience is just as interested in the actors conception of the role as they are in the play itself.

DW: Would you like to play in anymore mystery parts in the future?

BL: Yes, why not? I think they're very interesting but I would rather have it combined with some romance, it has a much greater appeal to the audience and even the box office or the producer would gain more.

DW: Speaking of romance, do you ever get to go to any Hollywood parties?

BL: No, life is too short for that. I wouldn't waste my time. There is too many interesting and wonderful things in the world that a man could achieve and experience. Besides, I don't even know how to play the . . . what do you call it . . . the uh . . . the ukulele!

D W: But you have so many friends, Mr. Lugosi.

B L: Well, I guess I'm pretty much of a lone wolf. I don't say I don't like people at all; but, to tell you the truth, I only like them if I have a chance to look deep into their hearts and their minds. If I find there's something, something worthwhile, some human kindness, some sympathy.

At this point, the interview turned into a parody of Dorothy West as a Dracula-like character.

In his book, *Horror: A Connoisseur's Guide to Literature and Film* (1989), Leonard Wolf summarizes Bela's portrayal of Murder Legendre

(The name of his character name in *White Zombie.*) in the following statement:

> ... we have Lugosi, slim as a rail, using hands and eyes, and even curiously bifurcated tiny chin whiskers like beautifully constructed implements of evil. He is the true death master, elegant, graceful and cold as ice at the North Pole.

In February 1933, Bela once again broke the hearts of his frenzied female fans when he escorted a beautiful, 20-year-old Hungarian maiden to Las Vegas and returned to Hollywood a few days later as a married man. The lady, who was the envy of Bela's female fans the world over, was Lillian Arch. In contrast to Bela's earlier romantic forays, this marriage lasted 20 years and produced one son, Bela Lugosi Jr. (a lawyer in Los Angeles).

Little is known about Bela's marriage to Lillian because he tried to keep his personal life extremely private and was very protective of Lillian (and Bela Jr.). Some have said he was possibly protective to a fault. Bela once said, "I think that marriage is like everything else. It's a matter of a good break, and I finally found a woman ... who is a mother, a goddess, a watchdog, a secretary, and a wife all combined in one."

Bela's first year of marriage to Lillian was a busy one. Aside from returning to the stage to star in a few dramas, he also made eight films. One of these films was his first serial (a serial was a film shown in chapters between the films of a double-feature). His first serial was supposed to be *Chandu the Magician*, with Bela playing Roxor, the "bad guy" in the guise of a mad doctor.

Chandu the Magician was originally filmed as a 13-chapter serial. During its preview, Fox Pictures realized they had a great film with considerable box-office potential. So, they filmed several additional segments to make the film complete. Then they released it as a full-length motion picture.

Chandu the Magician may not be the film for which Bela Lugosi is most remembered, but it is the one that garnered him much critical acclaim in 1933. It played in some of the nation's most prestigious grand theaters, although it did close rather quickly because of poor box-office receipts. *Chandu the Magician* also placed Bela in the company of such Hollywood luminaries as Charlie Chaplin, Clark Gable, Rudolph Valentino, Mary Pickford, Joan Crawford, and Greta Garbo. And, when a wax statue of Bela was displayed at the Motion Picture Museum and Hall of Fame, it was not modeled in the likeness of Dracula, Doctor Mirakle, or Murder Legendre. Bela's image was characterized as Roxor from *Chandu the Magician*.

As an dramatic artist, 1933 was a very busy year for Bela. Other than performing in various stage presentations, he appeared in the following films: *Chandu the Magician, Island of Lost Souls, The Death Kiss, The Whispering Shadow* (a serial), *Hollywood on Parade, International House, Night of Terror,* and *The Devil's in Love. Island of Lost Souls* was the most interesting film in Bela's career. But, the others certainly created more notches on his cinematic gun.

Island of Lost Souls starred Bela, David Manners and Edward Van Sloan, the same lead actors who starred in *Dracula*. KBS Films, the studio that produced these movies, took full advantage of this draw and promoted *Island of Lost Souls* as both a horror film (which it is not) and, inadvertently, a type of sequel to *Dracula*.

Bela filmed his scenes for *Night of Terror* during the breaks of *The Devil's In Love* and between performances of a Los Angeles stage production. In *Night of Terror*, Bela's magnificent eyes, once again, grace the screen.

In the *Night of Terror*, Cab Calloway performs the song *Reefer Man*, which promoted the use of marijuana. The song was originally cut from the film but has been recently restored for home-video viewing, although it is not included in the television version of the movie. This song inspired the anti-marijuana film *Reefer Madness* a few decades later.

It is obvious, from the reviews of most of Bela's films, he was attempting to land various types of characters in the roles he was choosing to play. However, he just could not escape the typecasting of his Dracula characterization.

Bela once commented:

> I am a victim of the success of *Dracula*. That horror drama and, along with it, myself have stumbled onto such great fame that producers and theater directors cannot even imagine that I could appear with a human face, too, and that I feel and believe that real art means talking with a human voice. I can't help it if they made a type out of me. The kind of role in which I have to work is completely foreign to my human and dramatic nature.

But, for the time being, I put up with my fate resignedly; I wear the clown's cap that I did not want at all.

Now it does not even surprise me that my name and mysterious profile have infected the entire United States to such an extent that wherever I happen to be, from Hollywood to New York, even the smallest villages, friendly strangers call me by name. Anyway, that is my livelihood and I have to wait patiently for the day that producers and theater directors realize that, after all, I am a man, too; someday I will get back the old roles that I played before Dracula, or, at least, roles similar to them where I will be allowed to appear on the stage as a human being and speak with a human voice. Until then, I carry and bear this heavy cross.

Bela's "cross" didn't get any lighter when he signed on to play the Sayer of the Law in the film *Island of Lost Souls*.

The question of why Bela accepted such a minor role, at this point in his career, is a matter of speculation. In *Island of Lost Souls,* Bela wears heavy make-up. (He is unrecognizable, unless you know his part, which consists of him repeating the same handful of lines throughout the film.) So, the question remains, why did Bela accept the role? Looking back, the only reasonable answer to this question is because he turned down the role of Frankenstein's monster. Thus, he created his own personal monster in the human form of Boris Karloff, and was terrified of repeating that mistake. This same conclusion can be applied to the other mediocre films Bela made during his acting career. Bela just could not say "no" to a role. He feared the monster he could create in his mind if he rejected a part offered to him. Regardless, *Island of Lost Souls* is a classic and a film worthy of every video library. (The original, unedited version was released on video, for the first time, in 1994.)

Island of Lost Souls, a film version of H. G. Wells' novel *The Island of Doctor Moreau,* outstrips the printed work in sheer dramatic effectiveness. It is an excellent film for many reasons: plotting, direction, stage sets – even acting. But, the source of its greatest power is the way that the Young-Wylie screenplay makes repressed or unacknowledged sexuality the absolute center of the film.

This film version of H. G. Wells' novel *The Island of Doctor Moreau* outstrips the printed work in sheer dramatic effective-

BELA LUGOSI: MASTER OF THE MACABRE

ness. It is an excellent film for many reasons: Plotting, direction, stage sets -- even acting. But the source of its greatest power is the way that the Young-Wylie screenplay makes repressed or unacknowledged sexuality the absolute center of the film.

What we have then is a story of linked erotic attraction . . . . Moreau, whose sexuality is very ambiguous, is in the throes of ecstasy as a voyeur whose delight is enhanced by the knowledge that he shares with the audience, that the love scene he is watching is tinged with beastiality. All of this heady stuff takes place in the foreground. In the background, there are the Beast People, all of them male, and their relationship to Moreau, their maker, and his House of Pain.

Laughton's performance is spectacular. His sutural face, adorned just by a bar mustache and a carefully sculpted anchor shaped beard, glows with a eunuch's passion . . . .

Then there is Bela Lugosi who, despite a face full of beard that almost completely hides him from sight, turns in a blood-curdling performance as he utters the law and then incites his fellow Beast Men to break it.

A triumphant film, at once laconic and beautiful, but most of all wise about the proximity of the instincts, animal and human, in the same body. And wise about Moreau's crime, which was to turn flesh into things.

Leonard Wolf
Horror: A Connoisseur's Guide to Literature and Film

One interesting aspect of *Island of Lost Souls,* it starred two of the biggest egos in Hollywood at that time: Bela Lugosi and Charles Laughton. Although it is not unusual for two such egocentric souls to cause enough friction on a studio set to create flames, this was not the situation surrounding Bela and Laughton. They actually got along splendidly. Between scenes, the two men would share wine and cigars. Shortly before his death, Charles Laughton commented on his career, in particular, *Island of Lost Souls.*

It wasn't the greatest film I ever made but it may have been the most interesting. I remember each horror and monster had more hair than the one before. Hair was all over the place. I was dreaming of hair. I even thought I had hair in my food . . . .

Working with Lugosi was quite fun as we both came from European training and had many tales to share with one another. I had heard he was a difficult actor to work with, but then again, the same people said that about me. I found him to be personable and professional and of course he had the best cigars in town and the worst wine – some Hungarian rot-gut stuff that would put hair on your palms – there I go about hair again.

Although *Island of Lost Souls* did not break box office records when it was released, the fault lies not with the film, but with the studio and the timing of its release. The same day *Island of Lost Souls* was released, another little film based on an ape who grows too large for a cage debuted: *King Kong*.

Island of Lost Souls was banned in England because it was too gruesome. In America, everyone found something appalling about it, or so it seems.

The two most notable reactions to *Island of Lost Souls* in America concerned the gruesomeness of the film and its anti-religious aspects. Those who faulted the film on religious grounds took exception to Doctor Moreau (Charles Laughton) claiming to be the incarnation of God (which Moreau, in a roundabout way, implies). Because he procreates via medical science and human experimentation, he was spewing forth evil and mocking all that Christianity stands for and holds dear.

After *Island of Lost Souls'* initial theatrical run, it was never released again; for a time, it was thought to have been destroyed. Because of the demand of film historians and the outstanding work of the American Film Institute (AFI), the film was found, cleaned and transferred to video. This resulted in a new generation to witness one of the truly great horror films of all-time. *Island of Lost Souls* still packs the same punch it did in 1933. (Its conclusion has lost none of its pure horror intensity through the decades).

In 1933, Bela had a banner year because he had appeared in so many films. But, he decided to make 1934 different. Bela had always preferred the stage more than the screen, so he took full advantage of his screen popularity. He accepted many starring roles in various theaters throughout the East and West coasts. Not all these roles were in horror productions.

"I regard the movies only as a means to the end," Bela noted. "I need the movies because I need the success they bring to my career, to get the roads cleared for serious work."

Because of his screen success and his mystique, when ever Bela performed on stage, he played to a standing-room-only audience. The-ater-goers didn't flock to see Bela the actor – they were there to see the man who personified Dracula. Some people may believe this bothered Bela; the fact is, his ego would not let it bother him. When Bela looked beyond the footlights of the stage, he was looking out at his fans, and fans meant money. It was truly that simple.

When he was in Hungary, Bela was involved in both governmental and theatrical politics. The extent of his involvement caused him the flee his homeland or else risk losing his life. In America, Bela never really got involved in governmental politics but the same cannot be said about his involvement in theatrical politics. His venture into American theatrical-political circles changed the entire motion picture industry, which is still evident today.

Between stage productions and away from the motion picture studios, Bela and other motion picture employees (from both sides of the camera) held secret late-night meetings to talk about how they were being treated by the various studios. After a few months of meetings, an alliance was formed. This alliance, or union, became known as the Screen Actors Guild. Bela has never been given the full credit he deserves for its creation. Bela put his entire career on the line to help his fellow actors. If the studios would have known of his involvement in forming the Guild, they would have blackballed Bela from the entertainment industry.

Academy Award winning actor Don Ameche once said:

> Though Bela is remembered for being Dracula and his great catalog of films, in our business he should be almost lionized for his work in putting together the Screen Actors Guild. He put his entire livelihood on the line for everyone in the profession, from actors to the boom operators. If he would've been caught, hell, he wouldn't even had been able to get a job mopping the floor of a theater or studio, let alone act in one.

While Bela worked to put together the Screen Actors Guild, he performed in stage productions. One of the productions in which he starred was a bastardized version of *Dracula*. Although Bela donned the black cape of Dracula for his portrayal, that was as close to the stage adaptation of *Dracula* as it got. It was a one-man show, with Bela performing a few of the more memorable scenes from the play and the film, and a few light comedy bits. Lillian was also in the production playing a few minor roles.

Every time Bela appeared on the stage, his thoughts went back to his theatrical days in Hungary. It was as if the hard wood of the stage was the door to his memory and the footlights its key. After one such stage production, Bela described these memories:

> I want to say that my heart yearns for the Hungarian language, Hungarian stage and Hungarian audiences who showed me so much loyalty in past years. You know, after the elegant atmosphere of the National Theater in Hungary, it was difficult to play Armand or the Prince in *Yellow Lilly* in Newark or Passaic. It was a real comedown for me and caused me to doubt my own ability. You have to play in Passaic to believe it. The difference between small, local theaters and Broadway is tremendous, and I am happy to be on a beautiful stage again. I really feel as if I were home now.
>
> I didn't really intend to appear in theater here in the United States. I wanted to get into movies. In Berlin, I was relatively successful in films, so I was sure that there would be more promise here where the movie industry is so much larger, but when I arrived, the film industry was in a depression and studios closed one after the other, so I directed Hungarian shows to wait for my chance in films.

Bela never repressed his Hungarian memories, to the point that outside of films, his only friends were other Hungarians and Hungarian nationals. The Lugosi household was often the site of Hungarian parties which featured the food and wine of the country, a place where the English language, whether for a party or otherwise, was second to Hungarian. This is another reason why Bela never mastered the language of the land he now called home.

In a 1934 interview with a Hungarian newspaper, Bela reflected on his Motherland and how much he missed it.

> I don't know how you feel, but I think I emigrated to America too late. I left Hungary 13 years ago. When I crossed the

Hungarian boarder, I thought I could start a new life in the West. I was determined to change countries and to blow up my bridges behind me. I resolved to forget about everything that was Hungarian – memories, feelings, and culture. But it seems that I deceived myself, for I came to realize that I could not start an entirely new life anywhere – not in Berlin, not in New York or Hollywood. Everywhere I was compelled to lead a Hungarian life. I couldn't stifle the feelings of homesickness in myself anywhere. Everywhere I had Hungarian friends; I devoured news from Hungary; I sought out Hungarian ties, a reawakening of my own Hungarian spirit; I needed a Hungarian heart. I will never suppress my Magyar nostalgia. We read English language newspapers but scour them for news from home. We are soldiers of the movie industry, but our hearts rally to Hungarian sponsored events. The papers here announce our successes, but our hearts leap at the thought – the hope – that perhaps our brothers and friends read of them in Hungary. This is nothing but our eternal identity as Hungarians who are thrown out into a foreign world. This is not red, white and green patriotism, but rather the immutability of our ties and emotions as Hungarians. Despite thousands upon thousands of miles that separate us from Hungary, the distance is bridged by our Hungarian thoughts and feelings.

Though Bela cherished his Hungarian roots and talked about his days in Hungary, in almost every interview, whether he was invited to or not, he was definitely more international in his film roles. Without a doubt, the most interesting international character Bela portrayed was Mr. Wong in the Monogram film entitled *The Mysterious Mr. Wong*. Imagine Bela trying to sound Chinese with a thick Hungarian accent. It is actually as amusing as it sounds!

Contrary to a popular belief, this film was not in the *Fu Manchu* or the *Mr. Wong* series. (Boris Karloff starred as Mr. Wong in the *Mr. Wong* films; both Bela and Boris played Asians.) *The Mysterious Mr. Wong* was simply a typical quickie release from Monogram Pictures -- made only for one reason – to take advantage of the name Bela Lugosi and the money that name brought with it.

During this era of filmmaking, there was a genre of pictures known as "Yellow Films," films with Asian characters, most notably Chinese. With the exception of *Charlie Chan, Mr. Wong* and a few other films, the majority of these films featured Asians as the "bad guys." *The Mysterious Mr. Wong* is a perfect visual description of the Yellow Film genre, it is also the epitome of racism.

For the filming of *The Mysterious Mr. Wong*, Bela was given a script with only his lines, but no stage directions. He had no directions for his physical movements. According to producer George Yohalem, there was a reason for this:

> We gave Bela full control over his movements and this was indeed a rarity in film. Why did we do this? Very simple. When it came to accentuating body movements with words, Bela was the master. You've heard the expression "poetry in motion?" When you watch Bela on film that is just what you're seeing – poetry in motion.

Bela's co-star in *The Mysterious Mr. Wong*, Wallace Ford, who plays a stereotyped newspaper beat reporter who wants to be the next Walter Winchell, enjoyed working with Hollywood's master of murder, mayhem, and the macabre.

> This was a fun film and most of the fun was due to Bela, at least in a roundabout way. Though we had a script to work with, we were all given pretty much free rein to ad-lib and we all did, except for Bela, he stuck by the script. Because of Bela's lack of our language, he was not getting any of the jokes I was tossing around and when I was tossing them his way in our scenes together, he would just look at me strangely, obviously not understanding anything I was saying, and simply repeat the lines he had memorized. Though he never said anything, I'm sure that by the end of filming he would have loved to break my neck or considering his most famous role, bitten it!

Although Bela's movie roles were taking on some variety, there were still some motion picture companies trying to lure him into more vampire films – sequels to *Dracula* without using the fabled Count's moniker. In 1935, Metro-Goldwyn-Mayer signed Bela to a similar role in *Mark of the Vampire*. This film reunited Bela Lugosi and Tod Browning – the team responsible for the original *Dracula* movie.

In the 1980's and 90's, Hollywood forgot what the word "originality" meant. Almost every film it reeled out seemed like a remake or a sequel. Perhaps the same thing could be said about *Mark of the Vampire*. It was a remake of Tod Browning's *London After Midnight* (1927), a classic film of the silent screen era starring Lon Chaney. How close was *Mark of the Vampire* to *London After Midnight*? It was almost a frame-by-frame identical twin, but with a new cast and sound. Although *Mark of the Vampire* was not the first remake in film history, it was the first to be a copy so much like the original.

The similarity of *Mark of the Vampire* to *London After Midnight* was not the original intention of the producers. According to the shooting script, penned by Guy Endore, one of the film's sub-plots was supposed to be about an incestuous relationship between Bela's character and the character portrayed by cinematic newcomer Carroll Boreland (as father and daughter). When the Metro-Goldwyn-Mayer studio heads noticed this, the screams could be heard across the state. After four rewrites, the studio approved the final shooting script, a clone of *London After Midnight*.

This film was blessed with a fine cast (Lionel Barrymore, Elizabeth Allan, Lionel Atwill, Jean Hersholt, Donald Meeks, Holmes Herbert). But, the real stars were James Wong Howe (cinematographer) and the entire make-up crew, including Bill Tuttlew, who recalled working under the direction of Tod Browning:

> The crew and I didn't like to work for director Tod Browning. We would try to escape being assigned to one of his productions because he would overwork us until we were ready to drop from exhaustion. Browning was ruthless. He was determined to get everything he could on film. If the crew didn't do something right, Browning would grumble, "Mr. Chaney would have done it better." He was hard to please. I remember he gave the special-effects men a hard time because they weren't working the mechanical bats properly. Though he didn't drive his actors as hard, he gave Lionel Barrymore a difficult time during a scene. Lugosi's performance, however, satisfied Browning. Unfortunately, I didn't get a chance to know Lugosi better as he was rather aloof. Lugosi did his own makeup for the film. I added the bullet hole wound in his head.

Figure 6 – Bela Lugosi and Carroll Boreland from The Mark of the Vampire. *This film was banned in some areas because of the incestuous innuendo. (Copyright © 1935 by Universal Studios, Inc. Courtesy of MCA Publishing Rights, a Division of MCA Inc. All Rights Reserved)*

Why was Bela spared Browning's ire? The answer is two-fold. First, it was Bela's performance as Dracula, directed by Browning, that garnered him, not only critical praise, but a monetary status which ranked him among the top directors of his era. Second, Bela's physical acting talents reminded Browning of Lon Chaney; to Browning, Chaney was nothing short of a god.

Metro-Goldwyn-Mayer's production of *Mark of the Vampire* was a major surprise in Hollywood. As one Hollywood gossip columnist wrote, "Why is M-G-M getting into spook films? A company whose romance and musical films fill theaters has turned to screams and shock. The question here is why?"

The answer is actually quite simple. Horror films meant big box-office sales. When the name Bela Lugosi was associated with a horror film – especially a vampire film – it meant incredible profits into the studios bank account. M-G-M, headed by Louis B. Mayer, was the shrewdest film production company in Hollywood. There was no way this company was not going to jump on this genre bandwagon, which began four years earlier with Universal Pictures. M-G-M was not disappointed with its artistic decision. *Mark of the Vampire* was a big hit and has become a cult classic.

So, "Why did Bela take a vampire role when he felt he was typecast after portraying the most famous vampire in film history?" An answer to that question can be found in an interview Bela gave in the mid-thirties.

> I'll be truthful and admit that the weekly pay check is the most important thing to me. Of course I enjoy my work. I haven't been an actor nearly thirty years without getting pleasure out of the profession. And with me it wasn't a sudden urge – acting. I studied at the Budapest Academy of Theatrical Arts for four years, and emerged with a degree before I finally made my debut in Budapest. And even then I didn't rate important roles. It took several years more of hard work in small parts before I attained stardom . . . . Although I'm afraid I'm typed by now, I'd like to quit the supernatural roles every third time and play just an interesting, down-to-earth person. One of these days I may get my wish.

In a separate interview, Bela concluded that he was a puppet of

Dracula, thus the reason he took on the vampire role in *Mark of the Vampire*.

> Where once I had been the master of my professional destiny, with a repertoire embracing all kinds and types of men, from Romeo to the classics of Ibsen and Rostand, I became Dracula's puppet . . . the shadowy figure of Dracula, more than any casting office, dictated the kind of parts I played . . . never, surely has a role so influenced and dominated an actor's personal life.

It is interesting to note that at the time when Bela gave this interview, he was starring in a film entitled *The Mystery of the Mary Celeste*. He played it straight, in a non-horror role as a crusty, old sea captain.

After his appearance in *The Mystery of the Mary Celeste*, British International Pictures offered Bela a contract. He would earn $25,000 per picture. It was the most lucrative contract that Bela had ever been offered, but he declined it. Bela said the reason that he turned down such a deal was because of his beloved dogs. According to press releases, Bela refused to go to England to make two pictures because the British government required that his dogs would have to be quarantined for six months before being allowed to live with him (this was indeed the law). Bela claimed he could not subject his dogs to such treatment or be without them for such a length of time. This story sounds plausible enough, although it is far from the truth.

The real reason Bela declined this lucrative offer from British International Pictures is because he had become a drug addict – a Sunset Boulevard junkie.

CHAPTER SIX

FALLING FROM GRACE

In his private life, he still remains as the strangest man in Hollywood . . . . For years Lugosi has lived in the film capital, but no one knows him. With his wife and son, he lives in a secluded house in the Hollywood Hills, barred to all except a few Hungarian countrymen . . . . Truly, he is a man who walks alone.

From a Hollywood tabloid story:

Dracula is dead and the chief celebrant at the obsequy is Bela Lugosi. Dracula is dead and Lugosi, who created the monster, hopes all memories of Dracula will die too. Dracula made Lugosi famous, and then, in true Frankenstein fashion, ruined him. That actor hopes now that he can go on being just an actor, not a horror-master. With the movies' genius for reincarnation, nobody was sure that Dracula had drawn his last evil breath until Universal began filming *Dracula's Daughter*. Lugosi isn't even in it . . . . So Lugosi seems to have shaken off Dracula's ghost.

Paul Harrison wrote this article for the *Long Beach News*. Although Mr. Harrison was writing about the film *Dracula's Daughter* (which did not have Dracula in it), he could have been writing the same thing about Bela the man (as opposed to Bela the actor). Between the years 1937 and 1939, Bela appeared in only one film. The man who was once one of the busiest actors in the business was now deemed "bad meat."

Bela had begun a rapid journey down the Hollywood has-been highway. There are two reasons for this decline. First and foremost, this was the time of the British ban on American horror films. Second, and unknown at the time, Bela had become a drug addict.

The British ban on American horror films was, for all intents and purposes, another revolutionary war on an artistic front. Universal Pictures felt the monetary bite worse than most other studios because they were the main American source of horror films. Other studios were also feeling the crunch because they all had horror films in production. On an individual basis, no actor felt the wrath of the British Board of Censors as much as Bela Lugosi.

"You have to understand that Bela, though he hated to admit it, was a horror film star," said actor Ralph Bellamy. "When the British ban came, Bela was just about unemployable. Though he was indeed a fine and talented actor, that damned Dracula haunted him so – no horror films, no Bela."

Even though the British ban on horror films was still in progress (it included most of Europe, as well as Great Britain), the genre was still being produced by the American film studios. The problem here, as far as Bela was concerned, was that the films were being produced on the lowest budgets possible. There was not even enough money to pay an actor of Bela's stature for a cameo appearance. This era gave birth to a new genre of American filmmaking known as "poverty row" films, the very same type of films perfected by Monogram Pictures. It was a company Bela would work for in the early 1940's, making a total of nine films.

Just how bad was this period for Bela? In his own words:

The mortgage company got my house. I sold one car and then the other. I borrowed where I could but who considered a jobless spook a good risk? By the end of 1937 I was at my wit's end. I was forced to go on relief.

In an interview with *Modern Screen* magazine, Bela elaborated:

I sat by the phone until I grew to the door. I haunted, as Dracula himself could not have haunted, agents, studios, casting offices, places where Lugosi might profitably be seen, be remembered. Horror, to me, is the moving picture of myself, an actor, struggling for another chance, a week's work, a day's work, a bit, an extra job. And knowing that the more I struggled, the more frantic and therefore the more obvious my squirming and gasping, the more I was defeating my own ends. The horror is knowing that you won't find anybody to give you a hand when you are down. A down-and-out actor is already a ghost haunting the corridors where he once walked a star.

"Forced to go on relief" refers to a subsidy Bela received from the Motion Picture Relief Fund, and not public assistance.

What happened to the money Bela had made while being one of the biggest actors in Hollywood? As fast as it had been handed to him, he spent it. Bela was the epitome of a flamboyant European gentleman. For him, everything had to be the best. He never looked at price tags. If he wanted it, he bought it. And, Bela had no mind for business and surrounded himself with business associates and agents who sucked more blood out of him than Dracula did from all of his victims. He created film deals which were much less lucrative than those of other actors of his caliber (and even less than actresses who were generally underpaid, about the same amount as bit players). You can understand how a bank account could go from the black to the red in a very short time.

To add insult to injury, Bela's ego was crushed. This was not the fault of Great Britain's ban on the American film industry. It was caused by Bela's mindset. Bela felt that what was going on across the Atlantic was a "ban on Bela." Whenever the British Board of Censors stated that "films of this character are suitable for exhibition to children under no circumstances," it was always a film Bela had starred in.

When things got to their lowest point, Hollywood's most famous (or infamous) gossip columnist, Louella Parson, decided to wield her power of the pen over the industry (she did in fact have power over the industry). She wrote the following statement in her three-dot column on January 8, 1938. Headed, "BELA LUGOSI JOBLESS," the paragraph read:

What's the matter with Hollywood producers when a fine actor like Bela Lugosi can't find a job! I happen to know that

Bela has been so down on his luck that he has been well – nigh – desperate. His wife just had a baby [Bela Lugosi Jr. was born on January 5, 1938] and there was no money forthcoming to pay for the doctor until the Motion Picture Relief Fund came to the rescue.

The British ban on horror films was only one occurrence responsible for Bela's stagnant acting career. The film community did not know then that Bela had become both an alcoholic and drug addict. Bela loved Hungarian wine and he preferred Egri Bikaver. This wine was not exactly crushed from the finest of grapes – more along the lines of rot-gut. In addition to alcoholism, he was addicted to morphine, methadone, demerol, barbiturates, paraldehyde, and formaldehyde (embalmers' liquid). His drug addiction started out innocently enough when painkilling drugs were prescribed to Bela for wounds he had received during the war in Europe. Entering his senior years and his hectic filming schedule contributed to an increase in pain, too uncomfortable to bear.

Either Louella Parson's article or the easing of restrictions in Great Britain on American horror films returned Bela to his place in front of the cameras. However, the Bela who now graced the flickering frames of the celluloid in the movie theaters was not the same man. He had aged and looked like a 57-year-old man whose health was declining. Gone was the debonair European gentleman whose grace and style had been the envy of all men and the fantasy of most women. The drugs and alcohol had taken hold and would not loosen their grasp, for 20 more years.

In the first year of Bela's re-emergence, he performed in four films (all released in 1939). Three of these films were low-budget "B" films, *The Gorilla, The Phantom Creeps*, and *Dark Eyes of London* (also known as *The Human Monster*). The fourth movie had him back in the grand theaters of the world. He co-starred with Greta Garbo, one of the grand dames of filmdom and his female counterpart in secretiveness, mystery, and rumor-mongering.

The Gorilla, a film adaptation of a Broadway production, was written for the Ritz Brothers. Bela played the part originally written for Peter Lorre. Because of a delay in filming (a law suit filed against the Ritz Brothers by Fox Pictures) and because Lorre had other film commitments, Bela was brought in.

Alan Dwan, director of *The Gorilla*, remembers:

The plot was altered to fit the comedic talents of the Ritz Brothers. They dominated the show. It wasn't a happy picture because we all knew the show wasn't going to be more than a programmer. Where an opportunity arose for a laugh, we would take it. As far as Lugosi was concerned, we all knew he was exploited for billing purposes. The role did not do justice to his enormous talents. He was a professional and it was a pleasure to work with him.

And how much did Bela receive for this part? Fox Pictures paid $1,200-per-week rental for the gorilla costume – which was more than Bela made for the whole film.

The Phantom Creeps was the last cinematic serial Bela acted in (it had a total of twelve chapters). The way it was produced broke all traditions in filmmaking. Most films and serials were shot on various sets, the action sequences were written specifically for these sets. *The Phantom Creeps* used action sequences from other films and newsreels. Probably the most interesting sequence was culled from the Bela and Boris film, *The Invisible Ray* where a man in a costume enters a pit. In *The Phantom Creeps*, this man is supposed to be Bela's character, however, it is actually Boris Karloff's character from *The Invisible Ray*.

The director of *The Phantom Creeps*, Ford Beebe, remembers this · serial and working with Bela:

> Because retakes were minimal because of the tight shooting schedule of serials, Bela got together with me to look at the script before filming started. He worried about forgetting his lines. As a precaution, he had his lines written on scraps of paper, most of which were out of camera range, in his pockets, and other parts of his clothing. But this was typical of Bela who was a fine, hard-working perfectionist.

Bela forgetting his lines was not a "typical" occurrence, but it became more prevalent because of his over-indulgence in both alcohol and drugs. Before Bela's dependency problems, he could not only memorize a script in a matter of days, but he could memorize multiple characters in multiple scripts – just as he was trained to do on the Hungarian stage.

Dark Eyes of London was a film by Pathe Film, Ltd., a British studio. An interesting point to note, it was released after the British ban on horror films. This "British" film was far more brutal and horrifying than the films questioned by the British Board of Censors.

Bela portrays two characters in *Dark Eyes of London* – the evil Orloff and the kind Doctor Dearborn. When in the guise of Orloff, Bela's voice and diction has that famous Hungarian melody to it. However, when he assumes the character of Doctor Dearborn, his voice changes. He speaks with a British accent which seems so real and proper that you'd swear it was a Shakespearean actor speaking those lines. Actually, it was. Bela's voice was dubbed over by the voice of O. B. Clarence, a British Shakespearean actor.

Ninotchka , the fourth movie on the list of Bela's comeback films, brought him into the grand theaters of the cinema. This classic highbrow comedy also starred Hollywood's most elusive legend, Greta Garbo.

Those who have studied the art of filmmaking are aware that *Ninotchka* is a great film. But, what many do not realize, this masterpiece was almost not made.

Bela's role in *Ninotchka* was not a large one; but, it was a non-horror performance. This was especially important to Bela; and, it was also important to director Ernst Lubitsch. He said, "People are so accustomed to him as Dracula, that I thought a sympathetic moment would surprise audiences as much as it did him."

Most of Bela's lines were curt, primarily because of his problem with the English language and partly because he had difficulty remembering his lines. He did have one somewhat lengthy monologue. Billy Wilder, who wrote the screenplay with Charles Brackett, found Bela's delivery of this piece amusing and one of several high points in the film. Bela's lines, as they were originally written in the script:

> If I told you what's going on in Constantinople right now, you wouldn't believe me. They are sitting there, those three, for six weeks, and haven't sold a piece of fur. This anonymous report was sent to me. They are dragging the good name of our country through every cafe and nightclub. [He reads:] "How can the Bolshevik's cause gain the respect among Moslems when your three representatives Buljancff, Ivanoff, and Kopalski, get so drunk that they throw a carpet out of their hotel window, and complain to the management that it didn't fly!" Unbelievable! It's an outrage!

Many praised Bela for his excellent delivery of these lines, spoken in such a dead-pan manner. However, the praise is unwarranted. Bela didn't really understand what he was reading; he didn't get the humor in what he was saying. So, to him, it was just a part of developing the plot.

Mystery surrounded both Bela and Greta Garbo, so fans curiously wondered how well these two legends got along on the set. "We are both racketeering in mystery," Bela noted. "She is mysterious by publicity and I am mysterious by trade. I thought she would be a spoiled badness, but she was not. I did not fall in love with her at first, but later yes. She is so damned human; it is wonderful."

During the same interview, Bela was asked about playing in a non-horror film. He countered: "I like horror parts. Sincerely I like them, but not exclusively. I like a little this, a little that – a little straight, a little character, a little everything. I would like to play a middle-aged romantic part – like Milton Sills used to play – a fellow of fifty maybe that is still open to romance in his limitations."

Bela didn't know at the time he was filming *Ninotchka*, or when it was released that it would be banned throughout most of Europe and Communist-bloc countries. Although in some cases, it was edited to the point that the story didn't make any sense. *Ninotchka* is a bedroom comedy, laced heavily with sex, sin and temptation. It is an international escapade that mocks the repressive bureaucracy and humorless mind of the Communists.

Italy banned the film as offensive to Communists. France banned the film, but approved it on appeal. Mexico's censor passed the film, but it was vigorously opposed by Mexican Labor, which contained a strong Communist element. Yugoslavia deleted footage showing a parade in Moscow. Estonia rejected the film. Lithuania rejected the film. Bulgaria rejected the film because it showed submarine warfare and satire on Communist Russia.

Regardless of the censorship problems *Ninotchka* encountered, it was by far the most artistic film Bela had ever appeared in (not to mention the most critically praised). At Academy Award time, *Ninotchka* was nominated for the following Academy Awards:

Best Picture
Best Actress (Greta Garbo)
Best Writing (Original Story: Melchar Lengyel)
Best Screenplay (Charles Brackett, Walter Reish, Billy Wilder)

Europe's banning of *Ninotchka* did not cause Bela any critical harm (or mental harm). Unfortunately, it did not break the Dracula-monster stereotype that he had become either. In taking the role in *Ninotchka*, Bela was hoping it would open new doors for his talents. It didn't. For some unknown reason, it made the macabre aura surrounding him grow even more dense. But, Bela was working once again .

From 1940 to 1945, Bela made 20 films. All of these were horror films, with the exception of two (*The Saint's Double Trouble* and *Black Dragons*).

The Saint's Double Trouble, one of the films in a cinematic series, starred George Sanders as the debonair spy known as the Saint (later it became the television series starring Roger Moore). In this film, Bela assumes another international characterization: that of an Egyptian.

Bela's mind may have been ravaged by his drug and alcohol dependency by this time. As mentioned before, he had difficulty remembering his lines. Fortunately, his stage and film presence was still obvious.

During the shooting of *The Saint's Double Trouble*, Bela left the friendly confines of the United States for a few weeks. He ventured across the Atlantic to England to do some promotional work for his films. This country, which almost ruined him with their ban on horror films, now welcomed him with as much aplomb as a major political figure. As Bela traveled through England, he saw firsthand the effect the war was having on this country. He also read about the war in the English newspapers to learn about what it was doing to the rest of Europe. This awareness brought out Bela's political opinions, views he had kept deep inside himself since he had first arrived in America.

Many immigrants who become citizens of the United States are extremely proud of their new homeland and often consider their patriotism a form of religion. To all those people who personally knew Bela, they would consider him a member of this group. He was Hungarian by birth; but, he was a citizen of America by choice. There was talk in some segments of the Hungarian-American community that Bela was a "closet" Communist. The editor of the California Hungarian newspaper *Californiai Magyarsagi*, Zoltan Szabados, believed this of Bela. He said, "There were many of us who really believed he was a Communist. He went to functions sponsored by the Hundred Days, a Hungarian Communist group, and he also associated with the Neuwald Brothers. They were proclaimed Communists."

On the other side, fellow actor and Hungarian, Peter Lorre, denounced Zoltan Szabado's comments:

> He's full of shit! Bela was as far from being a Communist as you can get. Yes, of course he associated with Hungarians who were Communists but not because of their political leanings, because they were fellow Hungarians! Hell, because you associate with Catholics does that mean you don't eat meat on Fridays? Because you associate with Jews, does that mean you don't eat pork? Hell, because you play a vampire, does that mean you drink blood? These sons of bitches who said Bela was a Communist were just looking to make news for themselves by using his name . . . and they did! But they were liars, every single damned one of them!

On September 28, 1940, Bela made a public political speech, one of the few. He spoke about the Hungarian community coming together for the betterment of both America and Hungary:

> California Hungarians have sensed that I always regard it as my duty to set aside party views of any kind and attend any worthwhile Hungarian event as a rank-and-file Hungarian. The people in our beloved Hungary are facing an immense crisis, and if the millions of Hungarians who live abroad – especially in America – do not get together to help our motherland, I am fearful that Hungary will again become enslaved.

If these false accusations of Bela being a Communist would have reared their ugly head a decade later, Bela, no doubt, would have been tarred, feathered, black-balled, and artistically hung from his thumbs on the fabled corner of Sunset and Vine. A decade later would have dropped him into the middle of the greatest witch-hunt since Salem – the ugly, hateful and infamous McCarthy hearings.

While the unsubstantiated and untruthful rumors of Bela's political leanings were being spread, he took on two films which would have him billed in the credits with Boris Karloff. Although *Black Friday* and *You'll Find Out* co-starred both Bela and Boris, they did not share the same scene in either film.

The following statement is about Bela's film *Black Friday:*

After an accident, a college professor is given a gangster's brain, and the surgeon encourages him to believe that he is the gangster so as to find hidden loot. It's a plot-packed melodrama which fails to provide the chills suggested by the cast, but passes the time agreeably enough. Lugosi was originally cast as the professor, but proved wrong for the part. Stanley Ridges replaced him and walked off with the movie.

Leslie Halliwell
Halliwell's Film Guide

In 1940, the horror film rage was diminishing. Because of this, Universal Pictures was willing to do almost anything to create interest in this film, which included signing both Bela Lugosi and Boris Karloff. Universal also invited the press on set to watch one of the film's most memorable scenes. According to the press release sent out by Universal, Bela was to be hypnotized for his death scene – an effort to bring a sense of realism to his dying. On this particular day, ladies and gentlemen from the press watched the death scene with notepads open, and pencils sharpened.

"I don't think I ever saw a man die so horribly on the screen. I nearly died watching him," said Arthur Lubin, the director of *Black Friday*.

Reporters wrote for their respective newspapers and magazines about Bela's trance and the way he followed the directions of the hypnotist, Doctor Many Hall. Actually, the press was duped (which was not an uncommon occurrence either then or today). Director Arthur Lubin was a studio shill. The movie-going public was ripped-off. Hall was a charlatan. Bela was NOT really hypnotized (Doctor Hall was not a hypnotist – he was a minister with the self-proclaimed title of Doctor of Divinity). It was Bela's pure acting ability that fooled the press and the public. He finally found the opportunity to show the human side of emotions through his diverse acting ability. His death scene was performed like he had been trained on the European stage.

From 1941 through 1944, Bela Lugosi was under contract to Monogram Studio and its miserly president, Sam Katzman. During this period, Bela made nine films for Monogram and eight films for other studios. It was common practice then for studios to lend actors to other studios in return for a fee. Between the years 1941 and 1944, all the films Bela made, which were not made for Monogram, had him co-starring in films for other studios. And, all of these movies were horror films. *The Wolf*

Man, produced by Universal Studios, went on to become a classic of the American cinema.

The Wolf Man is a horror melodrama about werewolves and witch-craft. According to legend, a young man returns to England from America to inherit his family's castle estate. After returning home, he is bitten by a werewolf and from then on assumes a dual personality; sometimes he's a human and sometimes he's a werewolf.

As fate would have it, in the last great horror film to feature Bela Lugosi, he played a Rumanian gypsy named, aptly enough, Bela (since the war, Bela's hometown of Lugos had become a part of Rumania, as had Transylvania).

Bela's role in *The Wolf Man* was not a large one, not by any stretch of the imagination. In the entire film Bela only speaks 31 words and is on-screen for less than five minutes. But, it is his character, aside from the wolf man himself, who is pivotal to the movie. Bela is the original lycanthrope (werewolf) who attacks Lon Chaney and causes him to become the ultimate toothy hirsute one (*The Wolf Man*). He is the one who graces the misty, dark skies of Wales whenever the moon is full.

The female lead in *The Wolf Man* was the beautiful actress, Evelyn Ankers. Because of her incredible talent for screaming in this film, Evelyn was given the nickname "the scream queen." Although, Bela's role was small and his time on the screen minimal, the Master of the Macabre left a lasting impression on Evelyn Ankers.

She recalls her thoughts about Bela from that time in the following statement:

> Bela Lugosi was a gentleman of the "old world." I think he admired my British accent, being a famous actor from the Hungarian Theater.
>
> I didn't recognize Bela when I met him out of make-up! We had been talking about this and that for quite some time when he ended the conversation by him saying how much he enjoyed working with me on *The Ghost of Frankenstein*. It hit me right then that the snaggle-toothed horrifying character that he played in the film was the same man. Quite a testament to the talents of Jack Pierce.
>
> In *The Wolf Man,* Bela wore a bushy wig and a gypsy mustache – but a year in between pictures is a long time to one in the profession. During that time you do not come into much

personal contact with your fellow cast members. In the theater you see each other in and out of make-up every day for the run of the play. But Mr. Lugosi was quite the opposite from his screen characters; he was refined, cultivated and charming. This transition is not an easy thing to do as an actor. I learned from first hand experience when I made *Weird Woman* a few years later, again with Lon Chaney, Jr. The studio made me the villain in that film! Every time I would try to work myself up to look evil, especially in the scenes with Anne Gwynne, I would scrunch my eye brows, try for a mean look. When I turned to Anne we would both become hysterical with laughter. The director, Reginald Le Borg, was very patient. I was never cast as the "bad guy" again. Much to the credit of Mr. Lugosi's acting ability, he could get "into character" instantly – the meaner the better!

Bela's role as Bela the Gypsy was not originally slated to be as small as it was when filmed. Bela did have physical limitations because of his advanced age. But those in power at Universal deemed his appearance in the film a necessity, regardless of the size of the role. There were two reasons for this. First was the value of having "Lugosi" in the credits, marquee, and publicity of a Universal horror film. Second, they knew he would bring an air of authenticity to his role, as he was basically playing himself in his younger days – days when he actually was a member of a gypsy acting troupe in his native Hungary.

Although Bela's few scenes in *The Wolf Man* set up the entire story for film, they were not the ones that held theater-goers on the edge of their seats and left critics in awe. It is the scenes where Chaney, as Larry Talbot, turns into the wolf man (that transformation from man to beast) that spellbinds the audience. Considering the year in which this film was produced (1941), the special effects for this transformation were truly incredible. Computer graphics or special effects wizards from Industrial Light and Magic weren't available at that time to map everything out – and Lon Chaney had to feel the brunt of the whole thing. Chaney tells just how was this incredible feat of special effects was accomplished in the following statement:

> The day we did the transformation, I came in at two in the morning. When I hit that position they would take little nails and

drive them through the skin at the edge of my fingers, on both hands, so that I wouldn't move them anymore. While I was in this position, they would build a plaster cast of the back of my head. Then they would take the drapes from behind me and starch them, and while they were drying them, they would take the camera and weigh it down with one ton, so that it wouldn't quiver when people walked. They had targets for my eyes up there. Then, while I'm still in this position, they would shoot five or ten frames of film in the camera. They'd take that film out and send it to the lab. While it was there, the make-up man would come and take the whole thing off my face, and put on a new one, only less. I'm still immobile. When the film came back from the lab they'd check me. They'd say, "Your eyes have moved a little bit, move them to the right . . . now your shoulder is up . . ." Then they'd roll it again and shoot another ten frames. Well, we did twenty-one changes of makeup and it took twenty-two hours. I won't discuss about the bathroom.

Once word leaked from the studio of the intricacies of the wolf man's makeup and special effects, the press converged on Universal Studios wanting the details in all its glorious and gory details. This wasn't just the Hollywood tabloid press – press representatives came from across the nation. On the morning of December 3, 1941, the New York *Morning Telegraph* informed everyone about the secrets which turned Lon Chaney into one of film's most vicious monsters (thanks to the genius and magical hands of Universal's master make-up artist, Jack Pierce, who also created Frankenstein's monster). According to the *Morning Telegraph*:

> Lon Chaney Jr., who for a long time was cast in conventional roles, finally is creating a character to equal any played by his late father, "the man of a thousand faces."
>
> Chaney has the title role in Universals' *The Wolf Man*, and is transformed by make-up artistry into one of the strangest characters ever seen on the screen.
>
> In a picture its makers hope will give audiences the shudders, Chaney will appear as a werewolf – half man, half wolf.
>
> The Task of turning Chaney from respectable citizen into a

werewolf fell to Jack Pierce, creator of Frankenstein's monster, the Mummy and others.

Pierce had considerable difficulty finding just what a werewolf looked like.

"I combed numerous histories of England without finding a practical description of a werewolf,' he said.

"About all I learned was that the legend began, and still persists, among the people of Wales who live around the ancient castles.

"Sometimes the wind produces sounds like the howling of wolves. Apparently the werewolf legend started with the noises."

Unable to find a workable description of a werewolf, Pierce designed one of his own. He started with a plaster bust of Chaney, practicing the application of yak and kelp hair on it before starting on the actor.

"It takes four hours to get the makeup on, and 45 minutes to get it off again. Getting it off doesn't take so long, but sometimes is painful, if the hair sticks too tightly."

A strange nosepiece aids the "wolf" illusion, and even ears, hands, and feet have to be hairy. The werewolf wears a shirt and trousers, so Chaney is spared having the rest of his body made up.

All of this publicity being shone upon Chaney, whom Universal had practically announced was the Master of the Macabre's heir apparent, did affect Lugosi's massive ego.

Outside of shooting their scenes together, Bela stayed clear of Chaney and spoke hardly a word to him. In later years, Bela grew to dislike Chaney to the point that he considered him, on a personal and professional level, on the same low plateau as Boris Karloff.

Many stories surround this classic: the strange and eerie happenings on the set, and the numerous physical confrontations between certain members of the cast. But, for the most part, these stories are only pieces of Hollywood folklore. There were only two known incidents of intrigue about the filming of *The Wolf Man*. Actress Evelyn Ankers was party to one and a witness to the other.

At the end of the picture, the werewolf is chasing me. I turn and see him for the first time and faint in his arms. Claude Raines comes out of the fog and Lon, the werewolf, drops me on the ground and attacks him instead. If I remember the sequence properly, after I am dropped into this chemical fog, I was to lie still for a few seconds until I heard "cut." I didn't hear "cut." They started to prepare for Lon to finish the fight scene with Claude Raines. Well, they forgot me in all the hustle and bustle of changing camera setups. I had been overcome by the fumes and passed out. Fortunately someone in the crew nearly tripped over me and I was saved.

Lon didn't make out so well either, for, in the next scene, Claude took a wild swing with the walking stick, which had a very heavy head – made from metal with the wolf's head – and it hit Lon in the face. Lon took pain very well, but poor Mr. Raines was almost overcome with the thought that he had actually done some violence to another person. Either that or maybe he used his exceptional acting talents and was getting even with Lon for something that Lon might have pulled on him.

After reading all that Lon Chaney went through to make the wolf man a legendary cinematic creature, it is interesting that Bela wanted the lead role of the wolf man for his own starring vehicle. He was willing to go through the vigorous hours of makeup and all the physical maneuvers this role required. The part was given to Chaney because Universal was aware of Bela's age (59), fragile health, and his drug and alcohol problems. Bela's health problems were no longer the secret they were less than a year earlier.

For the filming of *The Wolf Man,* Bela was on loan to Universal from Monogram. At Monogram, Bela was the star of his films – most of which are now considered cult classics; a few are quite entertaining. All, or so it seems, were produced on low budgets and it appears that they were edited by a person who took to scissors like Jack the Ripper took to knives.

Two of the strangest films in which Bela starred for Monogram were *Spooks Run Wild* and *Ghosts On the Loose.* Both films featured the East Side Kids (who later became known as the Bowery Boys). Although Bela always voiced his wish to play in comedy features, when he was given the chance in these two films, he failed. There are two reasons for his failure. First, as a serious actor, Bela had impeccable timing.

However, in a comedy he was erratic, his discomfort was quite obvious. Also, Bela's sense of humor was extremely highbrow and these two films were the exact definition of lowbrow. So, it was a cinematic fiasco. Second, Bela, the man who caused more fright than any other actor in the history of the cinema, was petrified of the East Side Kids.

William Beaudine, who directed *Ghosts On the Loose*, remembered quite vividly Bela's actions toward the rowdy New Yorkers who made up the East Side Kids.

> Usually on a film set, the cast members eat together, share stories and the like. With Bela it was always different; he was always a loner type of guy when it came to Leo, Huntz and the rest of the Kids. Not only did Bela leave the set after each scene, he made sure he had escorts. When I asked him about this, he told me, and he was dead serious, that he felt the Kids were going to rob and beat him – that they were nothing but a teenage gang. I laughed, but I tell you, he was dead serious.

Huntz Hall, who was the character Glimpy in the East Side Kids, actually worked up the nerve to introduce himself to the man who had scared him senseless in numerous trips to the movie theaters.

> I decided to go over to his dressing room and say "hello," remembered Hall. I knocked on the door and introduced myself. Bela was extremely cordial and we spent some time talking together. "Well, Mr. Lugosi, what do you think of the East Side Kids?" I said. Lugosi raised his eyebrows theatrically and said, "Scum!" But Bela was only kidding. The Hungarian actor took his acting very seriously and did not like to clown around on the set. But Bela had a great sense of humor! He loved to laugh, but not to be laughed at. That would make him more angry than anything."

Film review for *Spooks Run Wild*:

> I defy moviegoers not to gasp when they see *Black Dragons*. Never have I worked in a story so startling or so blood-chillingly shocking. See it if you dare!
>> Promotional quote by Bela Lugosi

When *Black Dragons* originally went into production, it was a film dealing with the real Japanese secret society known as the Black Dragons, a Mafia-type organization. Bela's original role was that of an American plastic surgeon sent to the Land of the Rising Sun to make some of the sought-after members of the Black Dragons look like Americans. (This was not a difficult task considering that all of the actors playing the members of the Black Dragons were Caucasian-American actors).

After Pearl Harbor was bombed and the United States entered World War II, Monogram decided to take full advantage of the political climate throughout the United States and had Harvey Gates (the writer) change the script, Bela's character, and the entire feeling of the film. Bela was now a Nazi plastic surgeon and the members of the Black Dragons were wartime saboteurs out to penetrate America. These changes were intended to feed upon the frenzy of the American people. The original story, a great thriller, was ruined. It was turned into a racist, propaganda-filled film with only one aim: to accelerate the hatred for Japan and of its people.

Bela's co-star in *Black Dragons* was Clayton Moore. Moore, a few years later, would ride into immortality on a horse named Silver as the Lone Ranger. Moore commented:

> Lugosi seemed like a nice man. He was very courteous, but he generally stayed to himself working on his lines. We shot awfully fast. Things were written off-the-cuff. William Nigh was always willing to change the script. But overall, Monogram was a very pleasant place to work. The actors received the respect they deserved there.

If Clayton Moore found Bela "courteous" on the set, he was the only one.

George Pembroke, a co-star in *Black Dragons*, recalled:

> I had heard of Bela's many moods, but I never expected what I saw. Here was a man who was definitely in his declining years as far as both talent and health were concerned, and he expected to be treated as if he was the greatest actor in the world. Every time he spoke it was "me" this or "me" that. I honestly don't believe he knew anyone else was on the set. And the way he treated others was really uncalled for. The only

person on the set he showed some respect toward was Mr. Katzman and I guess the reason Bela showed him respect was because Mr. Katzman signed his check – so I guess I can't really call Bela a fool.

Actor Stanford Jolly, a Caucasian who played the leader of the Japanese society of the Black Dragons, remembered the making of the film only somewhat happily.

> It was less than a two-week shooting schedule. Dialogue was being rewritten daily and it was hectic. I remember Lugosi and I didn't get along well at all, nor did he get along smoothly with any of his co-workers. It was a real challenge doing this Japanese character. I had to go through a two-and-a-half hour makeup session each day of shooting for a complete change of features, plus creation of a full beard. The makeup man was a real artist.

Regardless of how his fellow actors felt about him on a personal level, Bela did enjoy making *Black Dragons* and reveled in the evil character he portrayed.

> To portray a maniac offers a compelling challenge. I find, however, that once I have completed such a role, my interest in it immediately abates. As a matter of fact, chill drama holds no lure for me as a spectator. On the contrary and apparently as a release from my work-day life, I personally gain my theatrical diversion most delightfully from the frothiest of screen nonsense. A travel subject or a cartoon short, well-made and free from realistic thrill stuff, is frequently my choice on the film bill.

Bela, while sitting in a darkened theater, doubled over in laughter while watching Mickey Mouse or Betty Boop as they comically conquered their myriad of foils. If this is true, then it proves the age-old adage that "truth is indeed stranger than fiction."

Bella's other Monogram "poverty row" films speak for themselves:

The *Invisible Ghost*, a horror story, features Bela Lugosi in a dual-personality role, like Dr. Jekyll and Mr. Hyde. Six or so corpses point to the most obvious person in the household, Bela's character. This is the only film in American cinematic history where the murder weapon is a silk smoking jacket.

The virile male lead in *The Corpse Vanishes* was Tristam Coffin and his remembrance of this film details the strangeness in one of the film's eeriest scenes.

> Everything went smoothly until we got to the sequence depicting Lorenz [Lugosi] and the Countess retiring for the night. They slept in caskets instead of beds and when it came time to shoot the scene, Elizabeth Russell was frightened of lying in a casket and refused to do the scene, so we had to use a double instead.

In *Bowery At Midnight*, Bela kills off mobsters and buries them in labeled graves in the cellar. An assistant, who hates Bela, wisks away each of the murdered men and hides them in a cave.

The Ape Man is another hair-raising film which depicts a mad scientist who invents a formula that turns him into a beast. If the makeup Bela wears in this film looks familiar, it should. It's basically identical to what he wore in *Island of Lost Souls*. For *The Ape Man*, Bela applied his own makeup, which was usually the case for most of his low-budget films.

The *Return of the Ape Man* film was not a sequel to *The Ape Man*, though this is what Monogram wanted the public to believe – both stories are completely different. The opening scenes, which show the ice encasements rather realistically, did not actually use ice; the look was created by crinkling up cellophane and filming through it.

In the *Voodoo Man*, Bela played the role of a doctor, another zombie film, with John Carradine as the keeper of the zombies. There were many film critics of the time who dubbed the film "doo-doo Man." *Voodoo Man* was Monogram's cheap attempt at remaking the classic Lugosi film (and the best voodoo/zombie film of all-time) *White Zombie*.

As Bela's Monogram contract came to its end, so did his marriage to Lillian. In August of 1944, she filed for divorce. According to the court records, Lillian and her lawyer, Bela had caused her "great bodily pain and mental anguish, impaired her health, destroyed her happiness or any happiness in the home of the parties hereto, and made the same miserable and discordant."

Concerning Lillian's claims in the court records, there have never been any witnesses nor evidence that Bela caused her "great bodily pain." However, the mental anguish cannot be questioned. Because of his drug addiction, Bela's mood swings were now common. Bela's low income worsened the situation; he was making only $2,000 a month. This was incredibly low considering how many films he was making (plus his stage work).

Before the divorce was legally recognized, Lillian had second thoughts. (It has been assumed that she felt it would cause mental anguish to Bela Jr.; but, this has never been proven.) Instead of the pending divorce, there was reconciliation. Although it was not a loving marriage, it lasted another 10 years.

The status of Bela's drug problem at that time is not known. In his own words: "I used to inject the methadone in my legs, but I lost fifty pounds – from my 180 pounds down to 130 pounds – and my limbs became just strings of muscle."

The Body Snatcher, a true horror classic, was the last Bela and Boris duo film. The other four films Bela made during the span from 1945 through 1948 were all dismal failures. This dry spell in Bela's cinematic career made him readily available to go back to his true theatrical love – the stage. However, like the fictional vampire who always comes back from the dead, the role he was continually offered by stage producers was Dracula. Because of his financial situation, Bela had no choice but to accept them all.

Once Bela was back on the stage, the love he felt for his art revitalized him. Bela's reviews were usually reviewed with favor, and his treatment of his fellow actors was in kind. Veteran character-actor Simon Oakland was lucky to share the stagelights with Bela on the East Coast and fondly remembers the pairing.

> Bela was undoubtedly the most generous actor I had ever met. He was never parsimonious when it came to dispensing advice, and his patience was really difficult to understand; most actors of his stature become temperamental and impatient with less experienced people, but he coached everyone just like a stage director.

As Bela was traveling the nation performing in various revivals of *Dracula*, Hollywood lambasted his ego. Universal released *Son of Dracula* with Lon Chaney portraying the Transylvanian Count (for legal

Figure 7 – Lon Chaney Jr. as Count Alucard in Universal's **Son of Dracula.** *Bela was not even considered for this role and never forgave Chaney for taking it. Alucard is Dracula backwards. Because of legal ramifications, the name Dracula could not be used. (Copyright © 1943 by Universal Studios, Inc. Courtesy of MCA Publishing Rights, a Division of MCA Inc. All Rights Reserved)*

reasons he was called Count Alucard – Dracula spelled backwards) and *House of Frankenstein,* with John Carradine playing Dracula. In both instances, Bela was not even contacted about the role he had made legendary. The reasons why Universal never contacted Bela is not known. It obviously wasn't because of the money, Universal could have contracted Bela for Hollywood's version of minimum wage. It wasn't because Bela had lost his marquee value; the publicity circus surrounding Bela's return to his most famous characterization would have packed theaters worldwide. So, what was the reason? The answer to this question will probably never be found.

As 1948 rolled around, Universal Pictures was not thinking about starting another horror rage at the theaters. They had two other problems to think about – Abbott and Costello!

Bud Abbott and Lou Costello were, at one time, the most popular comedy duo in the history of the American cinema. Because the average attention span of a movie viewer is about 90 minutes, their popularity waned and so did the crowds which once circled city blocks. In a fit of pure genius (a commodity which was as rare in Hollywood as it is now), an idea filtered through the executive offices of Universal: what if they took the ideas of their two biggest film genres – horror and comedy – and combined them? This idea gave birth to one of Universal's biggest money-makers of the era and the greatest (in a critical sense) of Abbott and Costello's many films: *Abbott and Costello Meet Frankenstein.*

Unlike Universal's most recent cast for *Son of Dracula* and *House of Frankenstein,* their only choice to play Dracula in this Abbott and Costello film was Bela Lugosi. Bela was more than happy to once again don the ebony cape. (This was the last time he would do so on film – though he was buried wearing the very same cape).

Bela was delighted to play the vampire Count once again in a major motion picture. He said, "All I had to do was frighten the boys, a perfectly appropriate activity. My trademark stands unblemished." But, working with the likes of Abbott and Costello was more than a little unnerving for the physically and mentally fragile Bela.

Bela always took his acting very seriously (even in comedies). He was always well prepared, and considered ad-libbing as nothing short of an intolerable amateur activity. While working with Abbott and Costello, Bela had to put up with all of the traits he detested – not an easy task for him.

Charles Barton, the director of the film, half-jokingly remembered:

To be honest, there were times when I thought Bela was going to have a stroke on the set. You have to understand that working with two zanies like Abbott and Costello was not the normal Hollywood set. They never went by the script and at least once a day there would be a cast pie fight. Bela of course would have nothing to do with any of this. He would just glare at those involved with his famous deadly stare and the only emotion he would show physically was one of utter disgust.

True, Bela was not happy with the ongoing set activity, but when it came to his salary, he was elated. For the first time in many years, Bela was paid a salary which was not an embarrassment to his talents. For his last screen performance as Dracula, Bela was paid $1,500 per week plus a contract with a 10-week guarantee.

Because of the money Bela was making in *Abbott and Costello Meet Frankenstein*, the rave reviews his performance received from the critics, and the new fan base he was building, Bela felt a new dawn for his career was approaching. He did not know then that this new dawn was leading to a quick sunset or that this sunset was colored in ugly hues that would finally fade into the paleness of death.

CHAPTER SEVEN

THE FINAL BOW

The way you walked was thorny –
through no fault of your own.
But as the rain enters the soil,
the river enters the sea –
So tears run to a predestined end.
Your suffering is over Bela, my son
Now you will rest in peace.

Maleva (Maria Ouspenskaya) over the dead body
of her son Bela (Bela Lugosi) in *The Wolf Man*

When Bela returned to America from England after making the film
Old Mother Riley Meets the Vampire (originally titled *Vampires over
London*), his name had been brought up before the House Committee on
Un-American Activities (also known as the McCarthy Hearings). In an
effort to quell any rumors before they got out of hand, Bela immediately
wrote a letter to the chairman of this committee, Representative John
Wood. His letter read:

> My belief in the principle of democracy and personal free-
> dom is firm and unshakable. My entire life in America has been
> guided by these principles. I am unalterably opposed to the
> Communist menace against these ideals. Communist totalitari-

anism has always been abhorrent to me. I have never knowingly or willfully given it aid or comfort in any way.

During the war I was one of several artists of Hungarian birth asked to sponsor an organization. Shortly thereafter I learned the so-called Hungarian-American Council for Democracy was in reality a Communist front. I promptly resigned. It's high-sounding platform was deliberately phrased to avert suspicion from its true auspices.

My indignation at such deception impelled me to communicate with the FBI. I reported all I knew. My judgment proved correct. Four years later the Attorney General cited this organization as subversive and disloyal.

Actors are usually too busy to pay much attention to organizations that request their sponsorship. These are times of sharpening conflict between freedom loving people and Red Fascism. We must act and speak boldly against this brutalitarianism. I urge my fellow artists to carefully scrutinize groups before giving their endorsement, lest they fall into a Communist booby-trap.

Bela's letter was read before the House Committee on Un-American Activities, by Representative Wood. Once it was placed in the public record, the name of Bela Lugosi was erased from the chalkboard of Communism, once and for all.

About this time, Bela met Ed Wood Jr. and they became friends. Bela made three pictures; all are now considered cult classics. At least one, *Plan 9 From Outer Space*, is thought to be the worst film ever made.

The Bela Lugosi – Ed Wood relationship has been chronicled in the outstanding film *Ed Wood*, starring Johnny Depp as Wood and Martin Landau, in an Oscar-winning performance, as Bela Lugosi. Although this film was slanted more toward fiction than fact (nobody ever claimed that Hollywood knew the difference), one thing is true – Bela and Ed Wood were close friends.

The first film of the Bela and Wood series, *Glen or Glenda?*, was without a doubt the strangest of the three. That is, as far as storyline is concerned. It can be summarized in one word: transvestitism.

Although Ed Wood died in 1978, his popularity is stronger than ever. His cult-like following is not limited to any one particular age group or genre. Wood's strange personal life has been talked about for years; he was a cross-dresser. David Ward, an actor who frequently appeared in Wood's films, remembered Wood the filmmaker in 1978:

> It's a shame Wood died before he became famous; because, I think he'd be drinking it all in. He really wanted to leave his mark in the world of film; and, I think he would have taken fame any way he could have gotten it. If it took a cult centering around bad movies to make him famous, he wouldn't have minded.
>
> I've got to say this about Ed – his work may be far from great, or even good, but at least he made films. A lot of people out here, in Hollywood, have tried and tried to make movies, but have never been able to. He succeeded where many others have failed.
>
> And now his films are being shown everywhere. I know most people just watch these things to laugh at them, but they're paying good money to see them at revival theaters or to purchase them on video cassettes. So whether they realize it or not, it's Eddie who's having the last laugh.

Why the professional relationship between Bela and Wood turned personal after the completion of *Glen or Glenda?* is anyone's guess. Some believe that Wood idolized Bela, a man he had once watched in awe up on the silver screen who he now called his friend – a film fan's fantasy come true. Then some believed Wood considered Bela a "father figure." Regardless of the reasons why they became friends, the feelings they had for each other were mutual.

Because of the close relationship between Bela and Woods, Bela had a shoulder to cry on when his personal life began to match his professional life. In June of 1953, the divorce of Bela and Lillian was finalized. Bela's professional career had declined to the point that he was only paid between $500 and $1,000 a film. The judge ordered him to pay Lillian only $1 a month for child support and no alimony. And, what about savings and investments? All Bela had to his name was two undeveloped parcels of land at Lake Elsinore, two insurance policies totalling $1,500 in value, and an automobile (which was Lillian's because Bela had never learned to drive). The judge deemed that Lillian should receive just about all Bela owned because she would not receive any alimony. The worst part of the divorce, as far as Bela was concerned, was that Lillian received sole custody of Bela Jr. This broke Bela's heart.

Shortly before Lillian left the house for the last time, Bela wrote her the following letter:

Dear Lillian,

I cannot tell you in words what I want you to know, because I am afraid that I might break down. I love you very much. It is my wish that you be happy, but I see with an aching heart that at present you are unhappy and you don't want to live with me under the same roof. You want to leave me just when I have gotten rid of my addiction with the help of Alcoholics Anonymous. I will never agree to your leaving, but I cannot hold you back if you don't want to find out, anyway, from me how you feel about a completely changed Bela.

Actually, Bela's addictions were not cured then and he had never completed an Alcoholics Anonymous "class" to cleaning up his life. He lied in the letter for one reason; he truly loved Lillian and would have done anything and everything in his power to keep her. Ridding himself of his addictions was not within his power.

Shortly after Lillian left Bela, Wood experienced one of the most frightening nights of his life because of Bela's liquor and drug induced state of mind. The following account of this particular night is in the words of Ed Wood Jr.:

It was about two in the morning when I got a telephone call from Bela and he sounded very depressed. He told me he had to talk to me and wanted me to come over and bring a bottle of scotch. I told him that it was awfully late and he cried, "Eddie, I need to talk." The sound in his voice was desperate, so I headed over. When I walked in the front door I saw Bela sitting in the living room, tears rolling down his face and a gun pointed directly at me.

"Eddie," he said, "I am going to die tonight. I want to take you with me."

I slowly walked towards him and held out the bag I had. Looking him in the eye, I said, "Bela I've got the scotch here. Why don't we have a few drinks first?"

He got up and got a couple of glasses but he never stopped pointing the gun at me. I poured each of us some straight scotch and when we were just about finished with the first drink, Bela put the gun down and brought up a newspaper which was lying on the floor next to the chair he was sitting in.

"Eddie," he said to me, "I have just read an article in the paper that disturbs me very much. It makes me want to die."

"What could make you want to die, Bela," I asked, "when you still have so much to live for?"

"Some kids wrote to a television station that played *Dracula* and asked if Bela Lugosi is still alive." As he was telling me this, he was crying and it was tearing my heart out, but I didn't dare interrupt him. "The kids, they see my old movies. You know, Eddie, the kids are not dumb today like many would like us to believe. They know the pictures are not new. They can add! No wonder kids ask if I'm alive or dead. What do you think we can do about that Eddie? You are the writer. You are the promoter. How are you going to tell those kids that Bela Lugosi is not dead?"

I then told him about a film I was in the process of putting together, a horror film, and that I wanted him in it. He perked up a little, stopped crying and I took the gun, unloaded it and put it away.

The film that Wood talked about to Bela was *Bride of the Monster* – a typical Ed Wood low-budget film which was more amusing (although unintentionally) than horrifying. During the filming of *Bride of the Monster*, Wood finally realized just how bad Bela's addiction to drugs really was.

When we were shooting *Glen or Glenda?* and *Bride of the Atom* (later changed to *Bride of the Monster*), I knew that he was taking drugs quite often. One day he actually showed me his leg with over twenty Band-Aids on it. He looked at me with suffering eyes and said, "Eddie, these drugs are killing me." After what I had just seen, I could only agree with him. They were killing him. And when we edited *Bride*, it was easy to see the physical deterioration. We could barely match his scenes shot at the beginning of the production with those shot at the end. Bela's health was declining so rapidly that it almost looked like we had two actors playing the same part.

Why, would Bela be so bold as to show Wood the track marks on his leg where he had injected drugs into himself? It was a call for help; Bela knew he didn't have the strength to do anything about his problem alone. He knew, with Wood's help, that he might be able to toss this "monkey," that he had been carrying on his back for more than 20 years, behind into the hell from which it arose. And with the help of Wood, Bela did just that.

On April 21, 1955, 72-year-old Bela Lugosi, barely able to walk, stepped through the doors of the Los Angeles General Hospital. His request to the admitting nurse was simple: he wanted to be committed for treatment – he was tired of being a junkie.

Once the news of Bela's admittance into the hospital hit the Hollywood streets, the media vultures let the world know of Bela's problem in banner headlines:

BELA LUGOSI ADMITS HE'S USED DRUGS FOR 20 YEARS!
BELA COMMITS HIMSELF AS DOPE ADDICT!

The day after doctors at Los Angeles General Hospital gave Bela a physical, he went to court for a hearing before Judge Wallace L. Ware. Bela said to Judge Ware:

I've been using narcotics for 20 years. I don't have a dime left. I am dependent on my friends for food and a small old age pension. I am anxious to rehabilitate myself and decided this was the only way to do it.

After listening to Bela's plea for help, Judge Ware responded:

The court wants to commend you for this very courageous act of yours. It is commendable that you have come forward voluntarily wanting to cure your addiction to the use of drugs. After all, you are only seventy-two years of age. And it will be wonderful to get well and live the rest of your life as you should.

Then Judge Ware committed Bela to the Metropolitan State Hospital in Norwalk, California for drug treatment.

In contrast to other facilities, where today's celebrities go rid themselves of dependency problems, chic "spas" like the Betty Ford Clinic, the Metropolitan State Hospital was basically an enlarged mental ward with a staff of hard-nosed doctors and nurses (who were known to be extremely capable, with an outstanding success record). Getting off your drugs or alcohol, meant going "cold turkey," which resulted in immediate withdrawal symptoms. That is when Bela's addiction to embalmer's formaldehyde was first discovered. Alcohol didn't have any effect on him because of the drugs he was using; so, Bela would mix formaldehyde with fruit juices to get his "buzz."

For the first few days of Bela's treatment, he was not allowed any visitors. His only human contact was with the doctors and nurses who treated him. He became deeply depressed and cried uncontrollably. The only words they could understand between Bela's sobs was, "I'm going insane! I just want to die!"

When Bela was permitted to receive guests, Ed Wood was the first visitor.

> When I walked into the ward, he was lying on his bed. The minute he saw me, he grabbed me by the sleeve and pleaded with me to get him out of there. He said they didn't know what kind of person he was and that they didn't know what he needed to make him feel good. I think that he believed they would give him special consideration, which they obviously didn't. He told me all about the crazy people they locked him up with. He called them "alcoholics, nuts, and psycho-people." A phrase I remember him using all the time to describe them was "cuckoo crazies." He begged me with tears in his eyes to get him released, but I had to tell him that was impossible. It was.
>
> Anyway, I have to admit that he looked better physically even though he had only been in the hospital for a short time. Once he was away from the drugs and alcohol, his cheeks got fuller and he seemed stronger, but he kept telling me that if he had to stay in that ward for one more day he would lose his mind.

August 5, 1955, three months after Bela was committed to Metropolitan State Hospital, he was released. The doctors who treated him proclaimed him to be "drug and alcohol free."

While Bela was a patient at Metropolitan State Hospital, he received many letters wishing him well. He was grateful for each one of them. However, there was one well-wisher who sent Bela many letters, Hope. If Bela had kept all of his fan letters from the past, he would have recognized the name and the handwriting. Hope had been sending him letters ever since she first saw him and fell under his spell as Dracula.

Hope Lininger, a Pennsylvania native, had worked her way to Hollywood and ended up working at RKO Studios. Bela discovered who this mystery lady was when he noticed an RKO watermark on one of the letters. When one of Bella's friends contacted RKO, they had only one Hope on the payroll.

Hope remembers:

> I had seen him at RKO Studios when he made pictures there. At the time I was working in the cutting department. I decided that it was a good opportunity to meet him, but I didn't really. When it hit the headlines that he had gone to the Norwalk State Institution for his drug problem, I started writing to him, but I never signed my whole name. Bela had no way of contacting me, but one morning the phone rang and it was Mr. Lugosi. He said I should come to visit. The next Sunday I did and the following Monday he asked me to come over after work. Some reporters were there and Bela announced that we were going to be married. It floored me!

August 25, 1955, Hope Lininger became the fifth, and last, Mrs. Bela Lugosi. Why would Bela marry a woman he didn't really know, especially considering he was only 20 days out of rehab? It, obviously, was not love – at least not love as most married couples might define the word. Bela's words best explain why he married Hope:

> I have no money, my youth is gone and I am a sick man. It dawned on me suddenly that she believed in a higher power, such as I believe in, too. I realized she belongs to my class. We speak the same language.

With his new lease on life and a new marriage, Bela felt he was once again ready to tackle Hollywood and the world of the cinema.

Bela first film was *The Black Sleep*; he co-starred with Basil Rathbone, Akim Tamiroff, Lon Chaney and John Carradine. This was Bela's last film for a major studio (United Artists). Although he felt he was ready for the rigors of a major motion picture, the film's director, Reginald Le Borg, did not. Bela may have been cured of his addictions, but he was still a very sick man.

"Lugosi was practically a wreck," remembered Le Borg. "He had a man with him continually who had to hold him up. He was in very, very bad shape . . . ."

The Black Sleep presented an opportunity to deflate Bela's still enormous ego; he had a part with no lines. He played Basil Rathbone's mute valet.

According to Le Borg:

> Lugosi came to me all the time asking, "Herr director, give me more to do, I do not speak." I laughed, "Well, your tongue is cut out, I can't give you more!" I told him, "You can't do more, you're Basil Rathbone's valet and all you can do is stand next to him and nod." Finally, I compromised. I told him I'd put him in some shots where Rathbone was speaking . . . . He started to grimace while Rathbone spoke, that spoiled the shot. But to placate Lugosi, I took a couple of close-ups of him, knowing they would end up on the cutting room floor. But that satisfied him, and he thanked me.

Those behind the scenes while filming *The Black Sleep* weren't talking about Bela's ego or health. They were talking about one particular confrontation between Bela and Lon Chaney. Le Borg remembers:

> There was, I won't say hate, but a certain rivalry going on between Chaney and Lugosi from the Universal days when they both played Dracula. You see, Lugosi was the great Dracula, but then something happened at Universal and they gave the part to Chaney (this for *Son of Dracula*). There was a terrible rivalry between them before I even arrived at Universal. It came out on *The Black Sleep*. Chaney was sore at something Lugosi brought up and it nearly came to a fight. Chaney picked him up

a little bit, but put him down. We stopped him. We kept them apart quite a bit.

Bela starred in a few low-budget stage productions around Southern California between *The Black Sleep* and *Plan 9 From Outer Space*, his last film. Those who have viewed these productions were saddened by the sight of this once great actor, whose magnificent movements graced each character he created, lope around the stage like a zombie and mumble his lines with poor diction (the lines he could remember).

Dracula, is Bela's most famous film. However, Bela's last film appearance, *Plan 9 From Outer Space*, is his most infamous. Bela plays a ghoul in *Plan 9*, a film which has received only negative reviews.

Plan 9 From Outer Space has been called the worst film ever produced. How bad is it? The flying saucers were hubcaps and paper plates on strings – the strings are visible! Wood's budget for *Plan 9* (most he literally begged from friends or a local Baptist church) limited his production costs greatly. The stars worked for, by Hollywood standards, minimum wage. Wood was paid $350 a week and the actors received approximately $500 a week. Bela Lugosi did not receive the $500; he died before completing his first week of shooting.

In *Plan 9*, Bela's parts were all silent because he was then unable to speak coherently. Bela's voice is not heard; his emotions are acted out, like a mime, in this macabre melodrama. It's a truly sad end to an artistically impressive career, as a body of works.

Bela died four days into the filming of *Plan 9 From Outer Space*. Wood's shoestring budget couldn't fit another actor into the budget to redo the parts shot of Bela. Wood couldn't edit Bela's scenes because they were the focal point of the film. So, Wood hired his wife's chiropractor (Dr. Tom Mason) to fill Bela's role. Every time the script called for a frontal shot, Mason raised the cape over his face to conceal his true identity (although no one at the time was fooled by this switch).

The scenes toward the end of *Plan 9 From Outer Space* where Bela portrays one of the "undead" was actually rehearsal footage inserted into the film.

Bela died in his home at 5620 Harold Way in Hollywood. According to his widow:

> I went out shopping and came home around seven. When I left, Bela was reading a script for a new film Ed Wood was

Figure 8 – The original set that was built for Dracula *did not photograph well so the cast was moved to the soundstage of* Phantom of the Opera. *(Copyright © 1931 by Universal Studios, Inc. Courtesy of MCA Publishing Rights, a Division of MCA Inc. All Rights Reserved)*

going to make. When I came home from the market, I saw him in his chair and told him I was home. He didn't answer when I spoke to him, so I went over to him. I could feel no pulse. Apparently he must have died a very short time before I arrived. He was terrified of death. Toward the end he was very weary, but he was still afraid of death. Three nights before he died he was sitting on the edge of the bed. I asked him if he was still afraid to die. He told me that he was. I did my best to comfort him, but you might as well hold your breath with people like that.

A massive heart attack caused his death.

Upon his internment at Holy Cross Cemetery, Bela was laid in his coffin wearing the cape and neckpiece he wore in Dracula – as he had requested. To date, there has been no proof that he has risen during full-moon nights. However, there is some speculation that his spirit did not die when his earthly body did.

In life and in death, Bela Lugosi was and forever remains the MASTER OF THE MACABRE!

Bela, you're putting us on.

Boris Karloff at Bela's funeral

STAGEOGRAPHY

Some of Bela's off-Broadway productions from 1920 to 1927 are not listed because playbills were not printed for certain productions.

1. *Ocskay Brigaderos*
Writer: Herczegh
August 24, 1902

2. *Hazasodjunk*
Writer: Guthi
August 25, 1902

3. *Felho Klari*
Writer: Ratkay
September 18, 1902

4. *Kurucz Feja David*
Writer: Fenyes
February 10, 1903

5. *Maria Stuart*
Writer: Schiller
February 26, 1903

6. *Ezergy Ejszaka*
Writer: Feld
March 1, 1903

7. *A Denever*
Writer: Meilhac & Halevy
March 3, 1903

8. *Monna Vanna*
Writer: Maeterlinck
March 4, 1903

9. *Fedora*
Writer: Sardou
March 5, 1903

10. *Trilby*
Writer: Du Maurier
December 29, 1903

11. *Tartalekus Ferj*
Writer: Rakosi & Guthi
January 8, 1904

12. *Himfy Dalai*
Writer: Berczik
January 11, 1904

13. *Az Aranykakas*
Writer: Blumenthal & Kadelburg
January 14, 1904

14. *A Kereszt Jeleben*
Writer: Wilson
January 15, 1904

15. *Rang Es Mod*
Writer: Szigeti
February 17, 1904

16. *Egyenloseg*
Writer: Barrie
February 19, 1904

17. *A Vasgyaros*
Writer: Ohnet
April 6, 1904

18. *A Bajusz*
Writer: Vero
April 10, 1904

19. *Romeo and Juliet*
Writer: Shakespeare
September 2, 1910

20. *Aranyember*
Writer: Jokai
September 4, 1910

21. *Az Ingyenelok*
Writer: Vidor
September 4, 1910

22. *Az Obsitos*
Writer: Kalman & Bakonyi
September 5, 1910

23. *Kamelias Holgy*
Writer: Dumas
September 7, 1910

24. *Adolovai Nabob Leanya*
Writer: Herczegh
September 8, 1910

25. *Az Ordog*
Writer: Molnar
September 9, 1910

26. *Taifun*
Writer: Lengyel
September 10, 1910

27. *Bilincsek*
Writer: Reichenbach
September 16, 1910

28. *A Postas Flu Es Huga*
Writer: Buchbinder
September 18, 1910

29. *Amihez Minden Asszony Ert*
Writer: Barrie
September 20, 1910

30. *A Vasgyaros*
Writer: Ohnet
October 10, 1910

31. *A Kard Becsulets*
Writer: Kazaliczky
October 19, 1910

32. *A Csikos*
Writer: Szigligeti
October 23, 1910

33. *Szigetvari Vertanuk*
Writer: Jokai
November 1, 1910

34. *A Kormanybiztos*
Writer: Guthi
November 11, 1910

35. *Bank Ban*
Writer: Katona
November 12, 1910

36. *A Sasfiok*
Writer: Rostand
November 23, 1910

37. *A Balkani Hercegno*
Writer: Lonsdale & Curson
November 25, 1910

38. *A Balga Szuz*
Writer: Bastaille
November 30, 1910

39. *A Gyerekasszony*
Writer: Bokez
December 6, 1910

40. *Anna Karenina*
Writer: Guiraud & Tolstoy
December 17, 1910

42. *Richard III*
Writer: Shakespeare
December 20, 1910

43. *Baccarat*
Writer: Bernstein
January 8, 1911

44. *Narancsvirag*
Writer: Farkas
January 9, 1911

45. *Meguntam Margitot*
Writer: Wolf & Courtline
January 14, 1911

46. *Sarga Liliom*
Writer: Biro
February 25, 1911

49. *Lotti Ezredesei*
Writer: Stonne
March 7, 1911

50. *Othello*
Writer: Shakespeare
March 9, 1911

51. *A Jomadarak*
Writer: Raeder
March 11, 1911

52. *Az Aranylakodalom*
Writer: Beothy & Rakosi
March 15, 1911

53. *Robin Orvos*
Writer: Premary
March 16, 1911

54. *A Tolvag*
Writer: Bernstein
March 23, 1911

55. *A Vig Ozvegy*
Writer: Lehar
March 30, 1911

56. *Hamlet*
Writer: Shakespeare
March 31, 1911

57. *A Makrancos Holgy*
Writer: Shakespeare
April 2, 1911

58. *A Boszorkany*
Writer: Sardou
April 5, 1911

59. *Viola Az Alfoldi Haramia*
Writer: Szigligeti & Eotous
April 10, 1911

60. *A Becstelen*
Writer: Garvay
April 11, 1911

61. *Delibab*
Writer: Sumegi & Kun
April 21, 1911

62. *A Kivandorlo*
Writer: Herceq
April 27, 1911

63. *Elnemult Harangok*
Writer: Rakosi & Malonyai
April 30, 1911

64. *Botrany*
Writer: Bataille
May 2, 1911

65. *Babjatek*
Writer: Wolf
May 3, 1911

66. *A Sarga Csiko*
Writer: Erkel & Csepreghy
May 7, 1911

67. *Trilby*
Writer: Potter & Du Maurier
May 8, 1911

68. *A Tanitono*
Writer: Brody
May 9, 1911

69. *Az Allamtitkam Ur*
Writer: Bisson
May 11, 1911

70. *A Zseni*
Writer: Nagy
May 14, 1911

71. *A Sabin Nok Eirablasa*
Writer: Schonthon
May 17, 1911

72. *Anatol*
Writer: Schnitzler
May 20, 1911

73. *Anna Karenina*
Writer: Guiraud & Tolstoy
September 3, 1911

74. *Sarga Lilium*
Writer: Biro
September 18, 1911

75. *Az Elet Szava*
Writer: Schnitzler
October 7, 1911

76. *Sarga Lilium*
Writer: Biro
November 9, 1911

77. *A Gesak*
Writer: Hall
April 12, 1912

78. *Anna Karenina*
Writer: Guiraud & Tolstoy
August 22, 1912

79. *Sarga Lilium*
Writer: Biro
September 5, 1912

80. *A Yasgyaros*
Writer: Ohnet
January 5, 1913

81. *Az Ember Tragediaja*
Writer: Madach
January 6, 1913

82. *Mary Ann*
Writer: Zangwill
February 1, 1913

83. *Cyrano De Bergerac*
Writer: Rostand
February 3, 1913

84. *Maria Stuart*
Writer: Schiller
February 7, 1913

85. *Richard III*
Writer: Shakespeare
February 10, 1913

86. *Caesar and Cleopatra*
Writer: Shawn
February 21, 1913

87. *Aranyember*
Writer: Jokai
March 3, 1913

88. *King John*
Writer: Shakespeare
March 4, 1913

89. *A Szentivaneji Alom*
Writer: Shakespeare
March 4, 1913

90. *Az Ember Tragediaja*
Writer: Madach
March 5, 1913

91. *Tartuffe*
Writer: Moliere
March 10, 1913

92. *II Rakoczi Fogsaga*
Writer: Szigligeti
March 15, 1913

93. *A Boszorkany*
Writer: Sardou
March 16, 1913

94. *Hamlet*
Writer: Shakespeare
March 17, 1913

95. *A Faklyak*
Writer: Bataille
March 28, 1913

96. *Bizanc*
Writer: Herczegh
April 8, 1913

97. *Draghy Eva Eskuje*
Writer: Pekar
April 14, 1913

98. *A Fogadott Apa*
Writer: Duquesnal & Barde
May 2, 1913

99. *Hernani*
Writer: Hugo
May 8, 1913

100. *Kegyenc*
Writer: Teleki
May 16, 1913

101. *Faust*
Writer: Goeth
May 22, 1913

102. *Endre and Johanna*
Writer: Rakosi
May 28, 1913

103. *A Kamelias Holgy*
Writer: Dumas
June 3, 1913

104. *Visla*
Writer: Sziget
September 13, 1913

105. *Bolondok Tanca*
Writer: Birinszki
September 19, 1913

106. *King Lear*
Writer: Shakespeare
September 29, 1913

107. *Az Utolso Nap*
Writer: Balazs
October 3, 1913

108. *Az Attache*
Writer: Meilhac
October 23, 1913

109. *A Konvent Biztos*
Writer: Farkas
October 24, 1913

110. *Essex Grof*
Writer: Laube
November 8, 1913

111. *Maria Antonina*
Writer: Szomory
November 21, 1913

112. *Az Egvszeri Kiralyfi*
Writer: Szep
December 19, 1913

113. *Monna Vanna*
Writer: Maeterlinck
December 22, 1913

114. *Karacsony*
Writer: Gardonyi
December 23, 1913

115. *Eva Boszorkany*
Writer: Herczegh
January 1, 1914

116. *Matyo Lakodalom*
Writer: Garamszeghy
January 16, 1914

117. *Macbeth*
Writer: Shakespeare
January 30, 1914

118. *A Kolcsonkert Kastely*
Writer: Pekar
February 6, 1914

119. *Aesop*
Writer: Rakosi
February 20, 1914

120. *A Nok Baratja*
Writer: Dumas
February 24, 1914

121. *Fenn Az Ernyo*
Writer: Szigligeti
March 7, 1914

122. *Liliomfi*
Writer: Szigligeti
March 9, 1914

123. *Az Igazgato Ur*
Writer: Knoblauch & Coleby
March 20, 1914

124. *Egy Kerrier Tortenete*
Writer: Pakots
April 3, 1914

125. *A Vasgyarus*
Writer: Ohnet
April 13, 1914

126. *King John*
Writer: Shakespeare
April 27, 1914

127. *Julius Caesar*
Writer: Shakespeare
May 4, 1914

128. *A Tronkovetelok*
Writer: Ibsen
May 15, 1914

129. *A Peleskei Notarius*
Writer: Gaal
June 4, 1914

130. *Maria Stuart*
Writer: Schiller
April 10, 1916

131. *The Passion*
Writer: Unknown
April 15, 1916

132. *Hamlet*
Writer: Shakespeare
April 30, 1916

133. *Macbeth*
Writer: Shakespeare
May 2, 1916

134. *Othello*
Writer: Shakespeare
May 6, 1916

135. *Romeo and Juliet*
Writer: Shakespeare
May 10, 1916

136. *Szokott Katona*
Writer: Szigligeti
September 17, 1916

137. *Hamlet*
Writer: Shakespeare
September 23, 1916

138. *Henry IV*
Writer: Shakespeare
October 11, 1916

139. *Aesop*
Writer: Rakosi
October 14, 1916

140. *Zsuzsi*
Writer: Barta
October 27, 1916

141. *Don Carlos*
Writer: Schiller
November 10, 1916

142. *Egy Szegeny Ifju Tortenete*
Writer: Feuillet
November 22, 1916

143. *A Harom Testor*
Writer: Herczegh
December 9, 1916

144. *A Makrancos Holgy*
Writer: Shakespeare
December 19, 1916

145. *Unnepi Jatek*
Writer: Herczegh
December 30, 1916

146. *Komuves Kelemen*
Writer: Karpati & Vajda
January 12, 1917

147. *Az Ember Tragediaja*
Writer: Madach
January 19, 1917

148. *A Hadifogoly*
Writer: Hevesi
February 9, 1917

149. *A Partutok*
Writer: Kisfaludy
February 12, 1917

150. *King John*
Writer: Shakespeare
March 15, 1917

151. *Szentivaneji Alom*
Writer: Shakespeare
March 16, 1917

152. *Maria Magdalena*
Writer: Hebbel
May 19, 1917

153. *Nagymama*
Writer: Csiky
May 26, 1917

154. *Ahogy Tetszik*
Writer: Shakespeare
January 18, 1918

155. *Charlotte Kisasszony*
Writer: Lengyel
February 22, 1918

156. *Arva Laszio Kiraly*
Writer: Herczegh
March 3, 1918

157. *II Jozsef Csaszar*
Writer: Szomory
April 5, 1918

158. *A Kamelias Holgy*
Writer: Dumas
April 7, 1918

159. *Gorogtuz*
Writer: Hevesi
May 3, 1918

160. *Romeo and Juliet*
Writer: Shakespeare
June 7, 1918

161. *Bizanc*
Writer: Herczegh
November 9, 1918

162. *Richard III*
Writer: Shakyspeare
November 15, 1918

163. *Henry VIII*
Writer: Shakespeare
November 24, 1918

164. *Bagatelle*
Writer: Hervien
December 29, 1918

165. *Sancho Panza Kiralysaga*
Writer: Lengyel
January 10, 1919

166. *Az Ember Tragediaja*
Writer: Madach
April 8, 1922

167. *The Red Poppy*
Writer: Picard
December 20, 1922

168. *The Werewolf*
Writer: Lothar
July 15, 1924

169. *Arabesque*
Writer: Head & Tietjens
October 20, 1925

170. *Open House*
Writer: Golding
December 14, 1925

171. *The Devil in the Cheese*
Writer: Cushing
December 29, 1926

172. *Dracula*
Writer: Dean & Balderston
October 5, 1927

173. *Murdered Alive*
Writer: Murphy & Baxter
April 2, 1932

174. *Murder at the Vanities*
Writers: Carroll & King

175. *Tovarich*
Writer: Deval
March, 1937

176. *Dracula*
Writer: Dean & Balderston
May 3, 1943

177. *Arsenic and Old Lace*
Writer: Kesselring
August 5, 1943

178. *No Traveler Returns*
Writer: Goddard
February 26, 1945

179. *The Devil Also Dreams*
Writer: Rotter & Rohn
August 14, 1950

180. *Dracula*
Writer: Dean & Balderston
June 26, 1951

181. *Devil's Paradise*
Writer: Leong
June 8, 1956

FILMOGRAPHY

1. *Alarcosa* (Hungarian Film)
Star Films
Director: Alfred Deesy
1917
Cast: Arisztid Olt, Norbert Dan, Annie Goth, Robert Fiath, Richard Kornai, Viktor Kurd.

2. *Az Elet Kiralya* (Hungarian Film)
Star Films
Director: Alfred Deesy
1917
Cast: Arisztid Olt, Norbert Dan, Gustav Twian, Ila Loth, Annie Goth, Richard Kornai, Carmilla Hollay, Viktor Kurd.

3. *A Leopard* (Hungarian Film)
Star Films
Director: Alfred Deesy
1917
Cast: Arisztid Olt, Gustav Turan, Peter Konrady, Ila Loth, Klara Peterity, Anna Goth.

4. *A Naszdal* (Hungarian Film)
Star Films
Director: Alfred Deesy
1917
Cast: Arisztid Olt, Klara Peterity, Karoly Lajthay, Irene Barta.

5. *Tavaszi Vihar* (Hungarian Film)
Star Films
Director: Alfred Deesy
1917
Starring: Arisztid Olt, Norbert Dan, Aladar Fengo, Viktor Kurd.

6. *Az Ezredes* (Hungarian Film)
Phoenix Films
Director: Michael Curtiz
1917
Cast: Bela Lugosi, Zoltan Szeremy, Bero Maly, Laszlo Molnar, Sandor Goth, Arpad Latabar, Karoly Huszar.

7. *Casanova* (Hungarian Film)
Star Films
Director: Cornelius Hintner
Cast: Bela Lugosi, Anna Goth, Viktor Kurd.

8. *Lulu* (Hungarian Film)
Phoenix Films
Director: Michael Curtiz
1918
Cast: Bela Lugosi, Klara Peterity, Norman Dan.

9. *Kilencvenkilenc* (Hungarian Film)
Phoenix Films
Director: Michael Curtiz
1918
Cast: Bela Lugosi, Lajos Rethey, Zoltan Szeremy, Claire Lotto, Mihaly Varcony, Gyula Gal, Jeno Balassa.

10. *Sklaven Fremdes Willens* (German Film)
Eichberg Films
Director: Richard Eichberg
1919
Cast: Bela Lugosi, Lee Parry, Karl Halden, Violette Napierska, Margo Koehler, Gustav Birkholz.

11. *Nat Pinkerton* (German Film)
Dua Films
Director: Wolfgang Neff
1920
Cast: Bela Lugosi, Olaf Storm, Nestor Pridum, Marian Alma, Sybill de Bree, E. V. Meghen.

12. *Der Fluch Der Menschheit* (German Film)
Eichberg Films
Director: Richard Eichberg
1920
Cast: Bela Lugosi, Lee Parry, Willi Kaiser, Robert Scholz, Gustav Birkholz, Reinhold Pasch, Marga Koehler, Felix Hecht, Violette Napierska, Paul Ludwig.

13. *Der Janusskopf* (German Film)
Lipow Films
Director: F.W. Murnau
1920
Cast: Bela Lugosi, Conrad Veldt, Margarete Schlegel, Magnus Stifter, Will Kaiser,Margarete Kupfer.

14. *Die Frau Im Delphin* (German Film)
Gaci Films
Director: Artur Kiekebusch-Brenken
1920
Cast: Bela Lugosi, Emille Sannom, Magnus Stifter, Ernest Pittschau, Max Zilzer, Jaques Wandryck.

15. *Die Todeskarawane* (German Film)
Ustad Films
Director: Marie Luise Droop
1920
Cast: Bela Lugosi, Carl de Vogt, Mainhart Maur.

16. *Lederstrumph* (German Film)
Luna Films
Director: Arthur Wellin
1920
Cast: Bela Lugosi, Emil Mamelok, Herta Heden, Gottgried Kraus, Edward Eyseneck, Margot Sokolowska.

17. *Die Teufelsanbeter* (German Film)
Ustad Films
Director: Marie Luise Droop
1920
Cast: Bela Lugosi, Carl de Vogt, Meinhart Maur, Ilja Dubrowski.

18. *Johnann Hopkins III* (German Film)
Due Films
Director: Unknown
Cast: Not listed

19. *Der Tanz Auf Dem Vulkan* (German Film)
Eichberg Films
Director: Richard Eichberg
1921
Cast: Bela Lugosi, Lee Parry, Violette Napierska, Robert Scholz, Gustav Birkholz, Felix Hecht, Kurt Fuss.

(The following films were all American or British productions.)

20. *The Silent Command*
    Fox Pictures
    Director: J. Gordon Edwards
    1923
    Cast: Bela Lugosi, Edmund Lowe, Carl Harbaugh, Martin Faust, Gordon McEdwards, Byron Douglas, Theodore Babcock, George Lessey, Henry Armetta, Alma Tell, Martha Mansfield, Betty Jewel, Kate Blancke, Elizabeth Mary Foley.

21. *The Rejected Woman*
    Distinctive Pictures
    Director: Albert Parker
    1924
    Cast: Bela Lugosi, Alma Rubens, Conrad Nagel, Wyndham Standing, George MacQuarrie, Antonio D'Algy, Leonora Hughes, Aubrey Smith, Betty Jewel.

22. *The Midnight Girl*
    Chadwick Pictures
    Director: Wilfred Noy
    1925
    Cast: Bela Lugosi, Lila Lee, Gareth Hughes, Delores Cassinelli, Ruben Blaine, Charlotte Walker, John D. Walsh, William Harvey.

23. *Daughters Who Pay*
    Banner Pictures
    Director: George Terwilliger
    1925
    Cast: Bela Lugosi, Marguerite De La Motte, John Bowers, Barney Sherry.

24. *Punchinello*
    Famous Lovers Productions
    Director: Duncan Renaldo
    1926
    Cast: Bela Lugosi, Duncan Renaldo, Ronda Rainsford.

25. *How To Handle Women*
    Universal Pictures
    Director: William J. Craft
    1928
    Cast: Bela Lugosi, Glenn Tyron, Marion Nixon, Raymond Keane, Robert T. Haines, Bull Montana, Cesare Gravina, George Herriman.

26. *The Veiled Woman*
    Fox Pictures
    Director: Emmett Flynn
    1928
    Cast: Bela Lugosi, Lia Tora, Paul Vincenti, Walter McGrail, Josef Swickard, Kenneth Thomson, Andre Cheron, Ivan Lebedeff.

27. *The Last Performance*
   Universal Pictures
   Director: Paul Fejos
   1928
   Cast: Bela Lugosi, Conrad Veldt, Mary Philbin, Leslie Fenton, Fred MacKaye, Gustav Partos, William H. Turner, Andres Randolph, San DeGrasse, George Irving.

28. *Prisoners*
   First National Pictures
   Director: William Seiter
   1929
   Cast: Bela Lugosi, Corinne Griffith, James Ford, Ian Keith, Julanna Johnston, Ann Schaeffer, Barton Hesse, Otto Matiesen.

29. *The Thirteenth Chair*
   M-G-M
   Director: Tod Browning
   1929
   Cast:Bela Lugosi, Conrad Nagel, Margaret Wycherly, Leila Hyams, Holmes Herbert, Mary Forbes, Helen Millard, John Davidson, Joel McCrea.

30. *Such Men Are Dangerous*
   Fox Pictures
   Director: Kenneth Hawks
   1930
   Cast: Bela Lugosi, Warner Baxter, Catherine Dale Owen, Albert Conti, Hedda Hopper, Claude Allister.

31. *King of Jazz*
   Universal Pictur
   Director: John M   son
   1930
   Cast: Bela Lugosi, Paul Whiteman, John Boles, Laura LaPlante, Bing Crosby, Jeanette Loff, Glen Tyron, Merna Kennedy, Slim Summerville, Billy Kend, Brox Sisters, Marian Statler, Don Rose, Tommy Atkins.

32. *Wild Company*
   Fox Pictures
   Director: Leo McCarey
   1930
   Cast: Bela Lugosi, Frank Alberston, H.B. Warner, Sharon Lynn, Joyce Compton, Claire McDowell, Mildred Van Dorn, Richard Keene.

33. *Renegades*
   Fox Pictures

Director: Victor Fleming
1930
Cast: Bela Lugosi, Warner Batter, Myrna Loy, Noah Beery, Gregory Gaye, George Cooper, C. Henry Gordon, Clin Chase, Noah Beery, Jr.

34. *Oh, For A Man*
Fox Pictures
Director: Hamilton MacFadden
1930
Cast: Bela Lugosi, Jeanette MacDonald, Reginald Denny, Marjorie White, Warren Hymer, Alison Skipworth, William B. Davidson, Albert Conti.

35. *Viennese Nights*
Warner Brothers
Director: Alan Crosland
1930
Cast: Bela Lugosi, Vivienne Segal, Alexander Gray, Jean Hersholt, Walter Pidgeon, Louise Fazenda, Alice Day, Bert Roach, June Purcell.

36. *Dracula*
Universal Pictures
Director: Tod Browning
1931
Cast: Bela Lugosi, David Manners, Helen Chandler, Dwight Frye, Edward Van Sloan, Herbert Bunston, Frances Dade, Charles Gerrard, Jean Standing, Moon Carroll, Josephine Velez, Michael Visaroff.

37. *Fifty Million Frenchmen*
Warner Brothers
Director: Lloyd Baron
1931
Cast: Bela Lugosi, Olsen & Johnson, William Gaxton, John Halliday, Helen Broaderick, Claudia Dell, Lester Crawford, Charles Judels, Carmelita Geraghty, Nat Carr, Vera Gordon.

38. *Women Of All Nations*
Fox Pictures
Director: Raoul Walsh
1931
Cast: Bela Lugosi, Victor McLaglen, Edmund Lowe, Greta Nissen, El Brendel, Fife Dorsay, Marjorie White, T. Roy Barnes, Humphrey Bogart, Jesse De Vorska, Charles Judels, Joyce Compton.

39. *The Black Camel*
Fox Pictures
Director: Hamilton MacFadden
1931

Cast: Bela Lugosi, Warner Oland, Sally Eilers, Dorothy Revier, Victor Varconi, Robert Young, Marjorie White, Richard Tucker, J.M. Kerrigan, Mary Gordon, C. Henry Gordon, Violet Dunn, William Post, Dwight Frye, Murray Kinnel.

40. *Broadminded*
First National Pictures
Director: Mervyn LeRoy
1931
Cast: Bela Lugosi, Joe E. Brown, Ona Munson, William Collier, Marjorie White, Holmes Herbert, Margaret Livingston, Thelma Todd, Grayce Hampton, George Grandee.

41. *Murders in the Rue Morgue*
Universal Pictures
Director: Robert Florey
1932
Cast: Bela Lugosi, Sidney Fox, Leon Waycoff, Bert Roach, Brandon Hurst, Noble Johnson, D'Arcy Corrigan, Betty Ross Clark, Arlene Francis, Herman Bing, Charles Gemora.

42. *White Zombie*
United Artist Pictures
Director: Victor Halperin
1932
Cast: Bela Lugosi, Madge Bellany, Joseph Cawthorn, Robert Frazer, Jean Harron, Clarence Muse, Brandon Hurst, Dan Crimmins, John Peters, George Burr MacAnnan.

43. *Chandu, The Magician*
Fox Pictures
Director: Marcel Varnel & William Menzies
1932
Cast: Bela Lugosi, Edmund Lowe, Irene Ware, Herbert Mundin, Henry B. Walthall, Weldon Heyburn, Virginia Hammond, June Vlasek, Nestor Aber.

44. *Island of Lost Souls*
Paramount Pictures
Director: Erle C. Kenton
1933
Cast: Bela Lugosi, Charles Laughton, Richard Arlen, Leila Hyams, Kathleen Burke, Arthur Hohl, Stanley Fields, Robert Kortman, Tetsu Komai, Hans Steinke, Harry Ekezian, Rosemary Grimes, Paul Hurst, George Irving, Joe Bonomo.

45. *The Death Kiss*
World Wide Pictures
Director: Edwin L. Marin

1933
Cast: Bela Lugosi, David Manners, Adrienne Ames, John Wray, Vince Barnett, Alexander Carr, Edward Van Sloan, King Baggott, Harold Minjir, Wade Beteler, Barbara Bedford, Al Hill, Mona Maris, Lee Moran.

46. *The Whipering Shadow*
Mascot Pictures
Director: Al Herman & Colbert Clark
1933
Cast: Bela Lugosi, Viva Tattersal, Malcolm McGregor, Henry B. Walthall, Robert Warwick, Roy D'Arcy, Karl Dane, Lloyd Whitlock, Robert Koztman, Lafe McKee, George Lewis, Tom London, Ethel Clayton, Jack Perrin, Norman Feusier.

47. *Hollywood On Parade*
Paramount Pictures
Director: Lewis Lewyn
1933
Cast: Bela Lugosi, Mae Questel, Eddie Borden, Rex Bell, Dorothy Burgess, George Sidney, Charlie Murray, Gayne Whitman, Marie Prevest.

48. *International House*
Paramount Pictures
Director: Edward Sutherland
1933
Cast: Bela Lugosi, W. C. Fields, Peggy Hopkins Joyce, Stuart Erwin, Sari Maritza, George Burns, Gracie Allen, Edmund Breese, Lumsden Hare, Franklin Pangborn, James Wang, Sterling Holloway, Rudy Vallee, Colonel Stoopnagle, Rose Marie, Cab Calloway.

49. *Night of Terror*
Columbia Pictures
Director: Benjamin Stoloff
1933
Cast: Bela Lugosi, Sally Blane, Wallace Ford, George Meeker, Tully Marshall, Edwin Maxwell, Bryant Washburn, Gertrude Michael, Mary Frey, Matt McHugh.

50. *The Devil's In Love*
Fox Pictures
Director: William Dieterle
193_
Cast: Bela Lugosi, Victor Jory, Loretta Young, Vivienne Osborne, David Manners, C. Henry Gordon, Herbert Mundin, J. Carroll Naish, Emile Chautard, Robert Barrat, Akim Tamiroff, Dewey Robinson, Jobn Davidson.

51. *The Black Cat*
Universal Pictures
Director: Edgar Ulmer

1934

Cast: Bela Lugosi, Boris Karloff, David Manners, Jacqueline Wells, Lucille Lund, Harry Cording, Egon Beecher, Anna Duncan, Henry Armetta, Albert Conti, George Davis, Paul Weigel, Herman Bing, Luis Alberni, Michael Mark, King Baggott, Paul Panzer, John Carradine.

52. *Gift of Gab*
Universal Pictures
Director: Karl Freund
1934

Cast: Bela Lugosi, Edmund Lowe, Gloria Stuart, Ruth Etting, Phil Baker, Ethel Waters, Alice White, Alexander Woolcott, Victor Moore, Hugh O'Connel, Helen Vinson, Gene Austin, Tom Hanlon, Henry Armetta, Andy Devine, Wini Shaw, Sterling Holloway, Edwin Maxwell, Janes Flavin, Douglas Fowley, Chester Morris, Boris Karloff, Paul Lukas, Binnie Barnes.

53. *The Return of Chandu*
Principal Pictures
Director: Ray Taylor
1934

Cast: Bela Lugosi, Maria Alba, Kimball Young, Lucien Prival, Phyllis Ludwig, Dean Benton, Bryant Washburn, Peggy Montgomery, Wilfred Lucas, Cyril Armbrister, Elias Lazaroff, Dick Botiller, Murdock McQuarrie, Jack Clark, Joseph Swickard.

54. *Best Man Wins*
Columbia Pictures
Director: Erle C. Kenton 1935

Cast: Bela Lugosi, Edmund Lowe, Jack Holt, Florence Rice, Forrester Harvey, J. Farrell MacDonald, Bradley Page, Mitchell Lewis, Esther Howard, Selmer Jackson, Frank Sheridan, Oscar Apfel.

55. *Mysterious Mr. Wong*
Monogram Pictures
Director: William Nigh
1935

Cast: Bela Lugosi, Wallace Ford, Arline Judge, Fred Warren, Lotus Long, Robert Emmet O'Conner, Edward Peil, Luke Chan, Lee Shumway.

56. *Mark of the Vampire*
M-G-M
Director: Tod Browning
1935

Cast: Bela Lugosi, Lionel Barrymore, Elizabeth Allan, Lion Atwill, Jean Hersholt, Henry Wadsworth, Donald Meek, Jessie Ralph, Ivan Simpson, Carroll Borland, Holmes Herbert, Michael Visaroff.

57. *The Raven*
Universal Pictures
Director: Louis Freidlander
1935
Cast: Bela Lugosi, Boris Karloff, Irene Ware, Lester Matthews, Samuel Hinds, Inez Courtney, Ian Wolfe, Spencer Charters, Maidel Turner, Arthur Hoyt, Walter Miller.

58. *Murder By Television*
Imperial – Cameo Pictures
Director: Clifford Sanforth
1935
Cast: Bela Lugosi, June Collyer, Huntley Gordon, George Meeker, Henry Mowbray, Charles Hill Mailes, Claire McDowell, Hattie McDaniel, Allan Jung, Charles K. French, Henry Hull.

59. *Mystery of the Mary Celeste*
Hammer Films
Director: Denison Clift
1935
Cast: Bela Lugosi, Shirley Grey, Arthur Margetson, Edmund Willard, George Mozart, Ben Welden, Dennis Hoey, Gibson Gowland, Clifford McLaglen, Terrence de Marney, Herbert Cameron, Ben Soutten.

60. *The Invisible Ray*
Universal Pictures
Director: Lambert Hillyer
1936
Cast: Bela Lugosi, Boris Karloff, Francis Drake, Frank Lawton, Walter Kingsford, Beulah Bondi, Violette Kimble Cooper, Nydia Westman, Daniel Haines, George Renavent, Frank Reicher, Inez Seabury, Walter Miller.

60. *Postal Inspector*
Universal Pictures
Director: Otto Brower
1936
Cast: Bela Lugosi, Ricardo Cortez, Patricia Ellis, Michael Loring, David Oliver, Wallis Clark, Arthur Loft, Guy Usher, William Hall, Spencer Charters, Hattie McDaniell.

62. *Shadow of Chinatown*
Victory Films
Director: Bob Hill
1936
Cast: Bela Lugosi, Joan Barday, Herman Brix, Luana Walters, Maurice Liu, William Buchanan, Forrest Taylor, Charles King, James B. Leong, Henry F. Tung, Paul Fung, George Chan.

63. *S.O.S. Coastguard*
Republic Pictures
Director: William Whitney & Alan James
1937
Cast: Bela Lugosi, Ralph Byrd, Maxine Doyle, Herbert Rawlinson, Richard Alexander, Lee Ford, John Piccori, Lawrence Grant, Thomas Carr, Carleton Young, Allen Conner, George Chesebro.

64. *Son of Frankenstein*
Universal Pictures
Director: Rowland V. Lee
1939
Cast: Bela Lugosi, Basil Rathbone, Boris Karloff, Lionel Atwill, Josephine Hutchinson, Emma Dunn, Donnie Dunagan, Edgar Norton, Perry Ivins, Lawrence Grant, Lionel Belmore, Michael Mark, Caroline Cook, Tom Ricketts, Lorimar Johnson, Gustav von seyffertitz, Betty Chay, Edward Cassidy.

65. *The Gorilla*
20th Century-Fox
Director: Alan Dwan
1939
Cast: Bela Lugosi, The Ritz Brothers, Anita Louise, Patsy Kelly, Lionel Atwill, Joseph Calleia, Edward Norris, Wally Vernon, Paul Harvey, Art Miles.

66. *The Phantom Creeps*
Universal Pictures
Director: Ford Beebe & Saul Goodkind
1939
Cast: Bela Lugosi, Robert Kent, Regis Toomey, Dorothy Arnold, Edward Van Sloan, Eddie Acuff, Anthony Averill, Edwin Stanley, Jack C. Smith, Roy Bancroft, Forrest Taylor, Karl Hackett, Robert Blair, Jerry Frank, Dora Clement, Hugh Huntley, Charles King.

67. *Ninotchka*
M-G-M
Director: Ernst Lubitsch
1939
Cast: Bela Lugosi, Greta Garbo, Melvyn Douglas, Ina Claire, Sig Rumann, Felix Bressart, Alexander Granach, Gregory Gaye, Rolfe Sedan, Edwin Maxwell, Frank Reicher, Peggy Moran.

62. *Dark Eyes Of London*
Pathe Films, Ltd.
Director: Walter Summers
1939
Cast: Bela Lugosi, Hugh Williams, Greta Gynt, Edmund Ryan, Wilfred Walter,

Alexander Field, Arthur E. Owen, Julie Suedo, Gerald Pring, Bryan Herbert, May Haliatt, Charles Penrose.

63. *The Saint's Double Trouble*
   RKO Pictures
   Director: Jack Hively
   1940
   Cast: Bela Lugosi, George Sanders, Helen Whitney, Jonathan Hale, Donald MacBride, John F. Hamilton, Thomas W. Ross, Elliot Sullivan, Walter Miller, Ralph Dunn.

64. *Black Friday*
   Universal Pictures
   Director: Arthur Lubin
   1940
   Cast: Bela Lugosi, Boris Karloff, Stanley Ridges, Anne Nagel, Anne Gwynne, Virginia Brissac, Edmund MacDonald, Paul Fix, Murray Alper, Ray Bailey, Jack Mulhall, Joe King, John Kelly.

65. *You'll Find Out*
   RKO Pictures
   Director: David Butler
   1940
   Cast: Bela Lugosi, Kay Kyser, Peter Lorre, Boris Karloff, Helen Parrish, Dennis O'Keefe, Alma Kruger, Joseph Eggenton, Ginny Simms, Harry Babbitt, Ish Kabibble, Sully Mason.

66. *The Devil Bat*
   PRC Films
   Director: Jean Yarbrough
   1941
   Cast: Bela Lugosi, Suzanne Kaaren, Dave O'Brien, Guy Usher, Yolanda Mallott, Donald Kerr, Edward Mortimer, Gene Bryan, Hal O'Donnell, Alan Baldwin, John Ellis, Arthur Price, John Davidson, Wally Rairdon.

67. *The Black Cat*
   Universal
   Director: Albert S. Rogell
   1941
   Cast: Bela Lugosi, Basil Rathbone, Hugh Herbert, Broderick Crawford, Gale Snodergaard, Anne Gwynne, Gladys Cooper, Cecilia Loftus, Claire Dodd, John Eldredge, Alan Ladd.

68. *The Invisible Ghost*
   Monogram Pictures
   Director: Joseph H. Lewis

1941
Cast: Bela Lugosi, Polly Ann Young, John McGuire, Clarence Muse, Terry Walker, Betty Compson, Ernie Adams, George Pembroke, Fred Kelsey, Jack Mulhall.

69. *Spooks Run Wild*
Monogram Pictures
Director: Phil Rosen
1941
Cast: Bela Lugosi, Leo Gorcey, Huntz Hall, Bobby Jordon, David Gorcey, Sammy Morrison, Donald Haines, Dave O'Brien, Dorothy Short, Dennis Moore, Rosemary Portia, Guy Wilkerson, Angelo Rossitto, Joe Kirk, Jack Carr.

70. *The Wolf Man*
Universal Pictures
Director: George Waggner
1941
Cast: Bela Lugosi, Lon Chaney Jr., Claude Raines, Warren Williams, Ralph Bellamy, Patrick Knowles, Maria Ouspenskaya, Evelyn Ankers, Fay Helm, Forrester Harvey, J.M. Kerrigan, Doris Lloyd, Harry Stubbs, Harry Cording, Kurt Katch.

71. *The Ghost of Frankenstein*
Universal Pictures
Director: Erle C. Kenton
1942
Cast: Bela Lugosi, Lon Chaney Jr., Sir Cedric Hardwicke, Ralph Bellamy, Lionel Atwill, Evelyn Ankers, Janet Ann Gallow, Barton Yarborough, Doris Lloyd, Leyland Hodgson, Olaf Hytten, Holmes Herbert, Harry Cording, Michael Mark, Dwight Frye, Lionel Belmore, Lawrence Grant.

72. *Black Dragons*
Monogram Pictures
Director: William Nigh
1942
Cast: Bela Lugosi, Joan Barclay, Clayton Moore, George Pembroke, Robert Frazer, Stanford Jolley, Max Hoffman, Irving Mitchell, Edward Peil, Sr., Robert Fiske, Joseph Eggenton, Kenneth Harlan, Bernard Gorcey.

73. *The Corpse Vanishes*
Monogram Pictures
Director: Wallace Fox
1942
Cast: Bela Lugosi, Luana Walters, Tristram Coffin, Elizabeth Russell, Minerva Urecal, Kenneth Harlan, Vince Barnett, Joan Barclay, Frank Moran, Angelo Rossitto, Gwen Kenyon, George Eldredge, Gladys Faye.

74. *Bowery At Midnight*
   Monogram Pictures
   Director: Wallace Fox
   1942
   Cast: Bela Lugosi, John Archer, Wanda McKay, Tom Neal, Dave O'Brien, Vince Barnett, John Berkes, Ray Miller, J. Farrell MacDonald, Lew Kelly, Lucille Vance, Anna Hope, George Eldrege.

75. *Night Monster*
   Universal Pictures
   Director: Ford Beebe
   1942
   Cast: Bela Lugosi, Lionel Atwill, Irene Hervey, Ralph Morgan, Don Porter, Nils Asther, Leif Erikson, Fay Helm, Frank Reicher, Doris Lloyd, Francis Pierlot, Robert Homans, Janet Shaw, Eddy Waller, Cyril Delevanti.

76. *Frankenstein Meets the Wolf Man*
   Universal Pictures
   Director: Roy William Neill
   1943
   Cast: Bela Lugosi, Lon Chaney Jr., Ilona Massey, Patrick Knowles, Lionel Atwill, Maria Ouspenskaya, Dennis Hoey, Don Barclay, Rex Evans, Dwight Frye, Harry Tubbs, Adia Kuznetzoff, Jeff Corey, Torben Meyer, Doris Lloyd.

77. *The Ape Man*
   Monogram Pictures
   Director: William Beaudine
   1943
   Cast: Bela Lugosi, Wallace Ford, Louise Currie, Minerva Urecal, Henry Hall, Ralph Littlefield, J. Farrell MacDonald, George Kirby, Wheeler Oakman, Charles Hall, Emil Van Horn.

78. *Ghosts on the Loose*
   Monogram Pictures
   Director: William Beaudine
   1943
   Cast: Bela Lugosi, Leo Gorcey, Huntz Hall, Bobby Jordan, Ava Gardner, Rick Vallin, Minerva Urecal, Wheeler Oakman, David Gorcey, Stanley Clements, Billy Benedict, Sammy Morrison, Bobby Stone, Frank Moran.

79. *Return of the Vampire*
   Columbia Pictures
   Director: Lew Landers
   1944
   Cast: Bela Lugosi, Frieda Inescort, Nina Foch, Matt Willis, Roland Varno, Miles Mander, Ottola Nesmith, Gilbert Emery, Leslie Denison, William C.P. Austin, Jeanne Bates, Sherlee Collier, Donald Dewar, Billy Bevan, George McKay.

80. *Voodoo Man*
Monogram Pictures
Director: William Beaudine
1944
Cast: Bela Lugosi, John Carradine, George Zucco, Michael Ames, Wanda McKay, Ellen Hall, Louise Currie, Henry Hall, Dan White, Pat McKee, Terry Walker, Claire James, Ethelreda Leopold, Ralph Littlefield.

81. *Return of the Ape Man*
Monogram Pictures
Director: Phil Rosen
1944
Cast: Bela Lugosi, John Carradine, Frank Moran, Judith Gibson, Michael Ames, Mary Currier, Ed Chandler, Mike Donovan, George Eldredge, Horace Carpenter, Ernie Adams, Frank Leigh.

82. *One Body Too Many*
Paramount Cafe
Director: Frank McDonald
1944
Cast: Bela Lugosi, Jack Haley, Jean Parker, Bernard Nedell, Blanche Yurka, Douglas Fowley, Dorothy Granger, Lyle Talbot, Lucien Littlefield, Jessica Newcomb, Fay Helm, Maxine Fife, William Edmunds.

83. *The Bodysnatcher*
RKO Pictures
Director: Robert Wise
1945
Cast: Bela Lugosi, Boris Karloff, Henry Daniell, Edith Atwater, Russell Wade, Rita Corday, Sharyn Moffett, Donna Lee, Bill Williams, Robert Clarke, Mary Gordon, Jim Moran.

84. *Zombies On Broadway*
RKO Pictures
Director: Gordon Douglas
1945
Cast: Bela Lugosi, Wally Brown, Alan Carney, Anna Jeffreys, Sheldon Leonard, Frank Jenks, Russell Hopton, Joseph Vitale, Ian Wolfe, Louis Jean Heydt, Darby Jones.

85. *Genius At Work*
RKO Pictures
Director: Leslie Goodwins
1946
Cast: Bela Lugosi, Wally Brown, Alan Carney, Lionel Atwill, Anne Jefferys, Marc Cramer, Ralph Dunn, Robert Clarke, Philip Warren, Harry Harvey.

86. *Scared To Death*
Screen Guild Pictures
Director: Christy Cabanna
1947
Cast: Bela Lugosi, Douglas Fowley, Joyce Compton, George Zucco, Nat Pendleton, Roland Varno, Molly Lamont, Angelo Rossitto, Gladys Blake, Lee Bennett, Stanley Andrews, Stanley Price.

87. *Abbott & Costello Meet Frankenstein*
Universal–International Pictures
Director: Charles T. Barton
1948
Cast: Bela Lugosi, Bud Abbott, Lou Costello, Lon Chaney Jr., Glenn Strange, Lenore Aubert, Jane Randolph, Frank Ferguson, Charles Bradstreet, Frank Fenton, Joe Kirk, Clarence Straight, Bobby Barber, Vincent Price.

88. *Old Mother Riley Meets the Vampire*
Renown Pictures
Director: John Gilling
1952
Cast: Bela Lugosi, Arthur Lucan, Dora Bryan, Richard Wattis, Judith Furse, Philip Leaver, Maria Mercedes, Roderick Lovell, David Hurst, Hattie Jacques, Dandy Nichools, Arthur Brander, Ian Wilson, Graham Moffatt.

89. *Bela Lugosi Meets A Brooklyn Gorilla*
Jack Broder Productions
Director: William Beaudine
1952
Cast: Bela Lugosi, Duke Mitchell, Sammy Petrillo, Charlita, Murial Landers, Al Kikume, Mickey Simpson, Milton Newberger, Martin Garralaga, Ray Corrigan.

90. *Glen Or Glenda?*
Screen Classics Productions
Director: Ed Wood, Jr.
1953
Cast: Bela Lugosi, Lyle Talbot, Dolores Fuller, Daniel Davis, Timothy Farrell, "Tommy" Haynes, Charles Crafts, Conrad Brooks, Henry Bederski, George Weiss.

91. *The Bride of the Monster*
Rolling M Productions
Director: Ed Wood Jr.
1955
Cast: Bela Lugosi, Tor Johnson, Tony McCoy, Loretta King, Harvey Dunn, George Becwar, Paul Marco, Don Nagel, Bud Osborne, Ann Wilner, Dolores Fuller, William Benedict, John Warren, Ben Frommer.

92. *The Black Sleep*
    United Artist Pictures
    Director: Reginald Le Borg
    1956
    Cast: Bela Lugosi, Basil Rathbone, Akim Tamiroff, Lon Chaney Jr., John Carradine, Herbert Rudley, Patricia Blake, Phylis Stanley, Tor Johnson, Sally Yarnell, George Sawaya, Claire Carleton, Lovanna Gardner.

93. *Plan 9 From Outer Space*
    Reunold Pictures
    Director: Ed Wood Jr.
    1959
    Cast: Bela Lugosi, Gregory Walcott, Mona McKinnon, Duke Moore, Tom Keene, Vampire, Tor Johnson, Lyle Talbot, Dudley Manlove, John Breckinridge, Joanna Lee, Paul Marco, Conrad Brooks, Criswell.

BIBLIOGRAPHY

Anger, Kenneth. *Hollywood Babylon II*, E.P. Dutton, Inc., 1984.

Barnett, Buddy, & Copner, Mike. *Bela Lugosi: Then and Now*. Sonic Art Video.

Bergan, Ronald. *The United Artist Story*, Crown Pulishers, 1986.

Bojarski, Richard. *The Films of Bela Lugosi*, Citadel Press, 1980.

Bojarski, Richard & Beals, Kenneth. *The Films of Boris Karloff*. Citadel Press, 1974.

Cremer, Robert. *Lugosi: The Man Behind the Cape*. Henry Regent Company, 1976

Dooley, Roger. *Scarface to Scarlett: American Films in the 30's*. Harcourt, Brace, Jovanovich, 1981.

Dorian, Bob. *Bob Dorian's Classic Movies*. Bob Adams, Inc., 1990.

Douglas, Drake. *Horror*. The MacMillian Company, 1966.

Eames, John Douglas. *The M-G-M Story*, Crown Publishers, 1982.

Eastman, John. *Retakes*. Ballantyne Books, 1989.

Everson, William K. *Classics of the Horror Cinema*. Citadel Press, 1974.

Everson, William K. *More Classics of the Horror Film*, Citadel Press, 1986

Filmfax Magazine. No. 3. June 1986.

Filmfax Magazine. No. 18. January 1990.

Filmfax Magazine. No. 22. September 1990.

Florescu, Radu and McNally, Raymond. *Dracula: Prince of Many Faces*. Little, Brown & Co., 1989.

Gardner, Gerald. *The Censorship Papers*. Dodd, Mead & Co., Inc., 1987

Giannetti, Louis. *Understanding Movies*, Prentice-Hall, Inc., 1982.

Halliwell, Leslie. *Halliwell's Film Guide*. Charles Scribners' Sons, 1983.

Hirschhorn, Joe. *Rating the Movie Stars*, Beekman House, 1983.

The Horror Film. Cinebooks, Inc., 1989

Juno, Vale, V. & Andrea. "Incredibly Strange Films," *Search Publications*, 10, 1986.

Katz, Ephram. *The Film Encyclopedia*. Putnam Publishing, 1979.

Lennig, Arthur. *The Count: The Life and Times of Bela Lugosi*. G.P. Putnam's Sons, 1974.

Lloyd, Ann. ed. *70 Years at the Movies*, Crown Publishers, 1982.

The Look of Horror. Line Books, 1989.

Lucaire, Ed. *Celebrity Setbacks*. Prentice Hall, Inc., 1993

Maden, Clare Hayworth. *The Essential Dracula*. Crescent Books, 1992.

Maltin, Leonard. *Leonard Maltin's TV Movie & Video Guide*, Signet Books, 1989.

Martin, Mick & Potter, Marsha. *Video Movie Guide*, Ballantine Books, 1990.

McCarty, John. *Psychos*, St. Martins Press, 1986.

Mordden, Ethan. *The Hollywood Studios*. Simon & Shuster, 1989.

Newman, Kim. *Nightmare Movies*, Crown Publishers, 1988.

Peary, Danny. 1988. *Cult Movies*, Fireside Books: 3, 1988.

Phantom of the Movies. *The Phantom's Ultimate Video Guide*, 1989.

Riley, Philip. ed., *The Wolf Man*, Magic Image Filmbooks, 1993.

Riley, Philip, ed. *Frankenstein*. Magic Image Filmbooks, 1989

Roud, Richard, ed. *Cinema: A Critical History*. Martin Secker & Warburg Ltd., 1980.

Schatz, Thomas. *The Genius of the System*. Pantheon Books, 1988.

Searles, Baird. *Films of Science Fiction & Fantasy*. Harry N. Abrams, Inc., 1988.

Sennett, Ted. *Great Movie Directors*. Henry N. Adams, Inc., 1986.

Sennett, Ted. *Off Screen/On Screen Movie Guide*. Simon & Shuster, 1993

Silver, Allan and Ward, Elizabeth. *Film Noir*, The Overlook Press

Skal, David. *Hollywood Gothic*. W.W. Norton, Inc., 1990

Stanley, John. *Revenge of the Creature Feature Movie Guide*. Creature Large Press, 1989.

Sternfield, Jonathan. *The Look of Horror*. The Running Press, 1990.

Stuart, Ray. *Immortals of the Screen*. Bonanza Books.

Webb, Michael. *Hollywood: Legend and Reality*, Brown Little & Co., 1986.

Weldon, Michael. *The Psychotronic Encyclopedia of Film*, Ballantine Books, 1983.

Wiener, Tom. *The Book of Video Lists*. Madison Books, 1988.

Wolf, Leonard. *Horror: A Connoisseur's Guide to Literature & Film*, Facts-On-File Books, 1989.

APPENDIX A

Dracula is probably the greatest horror film ever produced is a point which can be argued. A point which cannot be argued is that *Dracula* is the most influential horror film ever produced. To prove this point, the films which were spawned by Bela Lugosi's film version of *Dracula* are listed below.

(These films are presented in alphabetical order in the decade they were released. Following the year of release is the title, studio, and director. It should be pointed out that as long as this list may be, it is only partial. Obscure foreign films and those from television have been omitted, along with a rather large assortment of Dracula-related films in the adult genre of filmmaking).

THE THIRTIES

1936
Dracula's Daughter
Universal Studios
Director: Lambert Hillyer

1935
Mark of the Vampire
M-G-M
Director: Tod Browning

1936
Jaws of the Jungle
Jay Dee Kay Pictures
Director: J.D. Kendis

1936
Preview Murder Mystery
Paramount Pictures
Director: Robert Florey

1936
The Macabre Trunk
Ezet Pictures
Director: Miguel Zacarias

1939
The Return of Dr. X
Warner Brothers
Director: Vincent Sherman

1933
The Vampire Bat
Majestic Pictures
Director: Frank Strayer

THE FORTIES

1949
Abbott and Costello Meet
  Frankenstein
Universal Pictures
Director: Charles Barton

1945
Crime Doctor's Courage
Columbia Pictures
Director: George Sherman

1943
Dead Man Walk
Producers Releasing Corporation
Director: Sam Neufield

1940
The Devil Bat
Producers Releasing Corporation
Director: Jean Yarbrough

1946
Devil Bat's Daughter
Producers Releasing Corporation
Director: Frank Wisbar

1946
Face of Marble
Monogram Pictures
Director: William Beaudine

1944
Gandy Goose in Ghosttown
20th Century Fox Pictures
Director: Mannie Davis

1945
House of Dracula
Universal Pictures
Director: Erle C. Kenton

1944
House of Frankenstein
Universal Pictures
Director: Erle C. Kenton

1945
Isle of the Dead
RKO Pictures
Director: Mark Robson

1944
Return of the Vampire
Columbia Pictures
Director: Lew Landers

1943
Son of Dracula
Universal Pictures
Director: Robert Siodmak

1945
Valley of the Zombies
Republic Pictures
Director: Philip Ford

1945
The Vampire's Ghost
Republic Pictures
Director: Leslie Selander

1947
Les Vampires
Studio unknown
Director: Henri Gruault

THE FIFTIES

1958
Curse of the Vampire
Shaw Brothers Pictures
Director: Ramon Estella

1957
Blood of Dracula
Universal Pictures
Director: Herbert L. Strock

1958
The Blood of the Vampires
Universal Pictures
Director: Henry Cross

1959
The Curse of the Undead
Universal Pictures
Director: Edward Dein

1957
Return of the Vampire
Keris Pictures
Director: B.N. Rao

1958
The Horror of Dracula
Hammer Films
Director: Terence Fisher

1957
Lust of the Vampires
Titan-Athena Films
Director: Riccardo Freda

1957
Old Mother Riley Meets the Vampire
Renown Pictures
Director: John Gilling

1959
Plan 9 From Outer Space
DCA Pictures
Director: Ed Wood Jr.

1958
The Return of Dracula
United Artists Pictures
Director: Paul Landers

1959
Uncle Was A Vampire
Embassy Films
Director: Pio Angeleti

1957
The Vampire
United Artists Pictures
Director: Paul Landers

1959
Vampire Man
Toho Pictures
Director: Nobuo Nakagawa

195_
The Vampire Moth
Toho Pictures
Director: Nobuo Nakagawa

1958
The Vampire's Coffin
Cinematographical Pictures
Director: Fernando Mendez

THE SIXTIES

1964
Batman Dracula
Filmmakers Cooperative
Director: Andy Warhol

1967
Batman Fights Dracula
Lea/Fidelis Films
Director: Leody Dias

1966
Billy the Kid Versus Dracula
Embassy Pictures
Director: William Beaudine

1960
Black Sunday
American International Pictures
Director: Mario Brava

1966
Blood Bath
American International Pictures
Directors: Stephanie Rothman &
Jack Hull

1969
Blood Beast Terror
Tigon Pictures
Director: Vernon Sewell

1966
Blood Fiend
Pennea Films
Director: Samuel Gallu

1969
The Blood of Dracula's Castle
A & E Film Corporation
Director: Al Adamson & Jean Hewitt

1965
Blood Thirst
Chevron-Paragon Pictures
Director: Newton Arnold

1965
The Bloodless Vampire
Journey Films
Director: Michael du Pont

1969
The Bloodsuckers
Chevron-Paragon Pictures
Director: Michael Burrowes

1961
The Bloody Vampire
American International Pictures
Director: Miguel Morayta

1960
The Brides of Dracula
Hammer Films
Director: Terence Fisher

1966
Carry On Screaming
Warner Brothers
Director: Gerald Thomas

1963
Castle of Blood
Woolner Films
Director: Anthony Dawson

1964
Castle of the Living Dead
Malasky Films
Director: Herbert Wise

1965
The Devils of Darkness
Planet Films
Director: Lance Comfort

1964
Dracula
Fimmaker's Cooperative
Director: Andy Warhole

1968
Dracula Has Risen From the Grave
Hammer Films
Director: Freddie Francis

1965
Dracula – Prince of Darkness
Hammer Films
Director: Terence Fisher

1969
Dracula Versus Frankenstein
Eichberg Films
Director: Hugo Fregonese

1967
Dracula's Wedding Day
Filmmaker's Cooperative
Director: Mike Jacobson

1967
The Empire of Dracula
Filmica Vergara
Director: Federico Curiel

1967
The Fearless Vampire Killers
Filmways Productions
Director: Roman Polanski

1962
Kiss of the Vampire
Hammer Films
Director: Don Sharp

1964
The Last Man On Earth
American International Pictures
Director: Ubaldo Ragona

1966
Orgy of the Night
Ed Wood Films
Director: A.C. Stephen

1966
Queen of Blood
American International Pictures
Director: Curtis Harrington

1962
Slaughter of the Vampires
Mercury Films Ltd.
Director: Roberto Mauri

1966
A Taste of Blood
Creative Films Ltd.
Director: Herschell Lewis

1969
Taste the Blood of Dracula
Hammer Films
Director: Peter Sady

1968
The Vampires
Columbia Pictures
Director: Frederico Curiel

THE SEVENTIES

1972
Alabama's Ghost
Ellman/Bremson International
Director: Frederic Hobbs

1974
The Bat People
American Internation Pictures
Director: Jerry Jameson

1972
Blackula
American International Pictures
Director: William Crain

1973
Blood
Walter Kent Films
Director: Andy Milligan

1973
Blood Couple
Studio unknown
Director: Bill Gunn

1974
Blood for Dracula
Bryanton Pictures
Director: Paul Morrisey

1970
Blood Lust
Monarex Films
Director: Marijan Vajda

1977
Captain Kronos: Vampire Hunter
Hammer Films
Director: Brian Clemens

1970
Count Yorga, Vampire
American International Pictures
Director: Bob Kelljan

1970
Countess Dracula
Hammer Films
Director: Peter Sasdy

1970
Curse of the Vampire
Scertre Industries
Director: Peter Wecksburg

1971
The Deathmaster
American International Pictures
Director: Ray Danton

1979
Dracula
Universal Pictures
Director: John Badham

1972
Dracula A.D., 1972
Hammer Films
Director: Alan Gibson

1975
Dracula & Son
Quartet Films
Director: Edouard Molinaro

1974
Dracula and the Seven Golden Vampires
Hammer Films
Director: Ray Ward Baker

1978
Dracula's Dog
Crown International
Director: Albert Band

1972
Grave of the Vampire
Entertainment Pyramid
Director: John Hayes

1970
Guess What Happened to the Count Dracula
Merrick International
Director: Laurence Merrick

1973
The House of Dracula's Daughter
Universal Entertainment
Director: Gordon Hessler

1972
I, the Vampire
Hipamex Pictures
Director: Leon Klimovsky

1973
The Lady Dracula
Blackburn Productions
Director: Richard Blackburn

1979
Love At First Bite
American International Pictures
Director: Stan Dragoti

1970
Lust for a Vampire
Hammer Films
Director: Jimmy Sangster

1979
Mama Dracula
Valisa Films
Director: Boris Szulzinger

1979
Nosferatu the Vampire
20th Century Fox
Director: Werner Herzog

1975
Old Dracula
American International Pictures
Director: Clive Donner

1973
Orgy of the Vampires
International Amuzement
Director: Leon Kilmovsky

1971
Return of Count Yorga
American International Pictures
Director: Bob Kelljan

1973
The Satanic Rites of Dracula
Hammer Films
Director: Alan Gibson

1970
The Scars of Dracula
Hammer Films
Director: Roy Ward Baker

1973
Scream Blackula, Scream
American International Pictures
Director: Bob Kelljan

1973
Son of Dracula
Apple Films
Director: Freddie Francis

1974
Tender Dracula
Renn Productions
Director: Alaine Robbe Grillet

1974
The Thirsty Dead
International Amusement
Director: Terry Becker

1971
Twins of Evil
Hammer Films
Director: John Hough

1972
Vampire Circus
Hammer Films
Director: Robert Young

1971
The Vampire Happening
Aquila Enterprises
Director: Freddie Francis

1979
The Vampire Hookers
Capricorn Three Pictures
Director: Cirio Santiago

1970
The Vampire Lovers
Hammer Films
Director: Roy Ward Baker

THE EIGHTIES

1988
Beverly Hills Vamp
American International Pictures
Director: Fred Olen Ray

1988
Black Vampire
Kelly–Jordan Enterprises
Director: Lawrence Jordan

1980
Doctor Dracula
Independent- International
Director: Al Adamson & Paul Aratow

1980
Dracula's Last Rites
New Empire Features
Director: Demonic Paris

1988
Dracula's Widow
De Laurentis Entertainment
Director: Christopher Coppola

1985
Fright Night
Columbia Pictures
Director: Tom Holland

1989
Fright Night II
Heritage Films Ltd.
Director: Norman Thaddeus Vane

1983
The Hunger
M-G-M
Director: Tony Scott

1984
I Married A Vampire
Full Moon Productions
Director: Jay Raskin

1987
The Lost Boys
Warner -Brothers
Director: Joel Schumacher

1987
The Monster Squad
Taft Entertainment Pictures
Director: Fred Dekker

1987
My Best Friend Is A Vampire
Kings Road Entertainment
Director: Jimmy Houston

1985
Once Bitten
Samuel Goldwyn Company
Director: Howard Storm

1989
Sundown: The Vampire in Retreat
Vastrom International
Director: Anthony Hickox

1989
Teen Vamp
New World Pictures
Director: Samuel Bradford

1985
Transylvania 6-5000
New World Pictures
Director: Rudy De Luca

1989
Transyvania Twist
New Horizons
Director: Jim Wynorski

1986
Vamp
New World Pictures
Director: Richard Wenk

1988
Vampire at Midnight
Skouras Pictures
Director: Gregory McClatchy

1989
Vampire's Kiss
Hemsdale Film Corporation
Director: Robert Bierman

1988
Vampires on Bikini Beach
Beacon Films
Director: Jerry Brady

THE NINETIES
1990
The Arrival
Del Mar Entertainment
Director: David Schmoeller

1992
Bram Stoker's Dracula
Columbia Pictures
Director: Francis Ford Coppola

1992
Buffy the Vampire Slayer
20th Century Fox
Director: Fran Rubel Kuzui

1992
Dracula Rising
Concorde Pictures
Director: Fred Gallo

1994
Interview With A Vampire
Warner Brothers
Director: Neil Jordon

1991
My Grandpa Is A Vampire
Moonrise Productions
Director: David Blyth

1992
To Sleep With A Vampire
Concorde Pictures
Director: Adam Friendman

APPENDIX B

With all of the aforementioned films which came from the literary loins of Count Dracula and have made it the most "copied" film in the history of the world cinema, it can also be concluded that Bela Lugosi's incredible characterization of Dracula is the most "mimiced" fictional character ever brought to the silver screens of the world. The following 65 names have all donned the nocturnal ebony cape since Bela handed it down in 1931 Of special interest are eight names; the eight women who have played the evil Count in all of their feminine horror (yes, the role of Count Dracula has been an equal opportunity characterization).

For those into statistics, here's one no other cinematic character can proclaim: between the years 1931 to 1995, the character of Dracula has appeared, in one way or the other, 6.6 times a year in a motion picture (and considerably more if we were to include television, broadway and radio dramas).

Carlos Agasti
Christopher Atkins
David Avizu
Christopher Bernau
John Carradine
Eric del Castillo
Lon Chaney Jr.
Peter Cushing
Alex D.Arcy
Mitch Evans
Marty Feldman
Enrique Alvarez Felix
Fabian Forte

Lesley Gibb*
Jaime Gillis
George Hamilton
Patricia Lee Hammond*
Atif Kaptan
Vince Kelly
Udo Kier
Chimi Kim
Klaus Kinski
Mori Kishida
Suzanne Krazna*
Evelyn Kraft*
Paul Albert Krumm

Geoffrey Land
Frank Langella
Francis Lederer
Christopher Lee
Fred Lewis
Peter Loewy
William Marshall
Ferdy Mayne
Narciso Ibanez Menta Aldo Monti
Paul Naschy
Britt Nichols*
David Niven
Masumi Okada
Miles O'Keefe
Gary Oldman
Rossana Ortiz*
Jim Parker
Gabby Paul
Ingrid Pitt*

Dennis Price
Edmund Purdom
Duncan Regehr
Michael Rennie
Dante Rivero
Des Roberts
John Forbes Robertson
Tina Romero*
Cesar Silva
Jack Smith
Jeffery Smithers
Kostas Soumas
Kang Young Suk
Huni Tanaka
Dante Varona
Howard Vernon
Carlos Villarias
Zandor Vorkov
Norman Welsh

(*Denotes actresses who have played Dracula.)

INDEX

A

Abbott and Costello, 150, 151
Abbott and Costello Meet Franken-stein, 150, 151
Abbott, Bud, 150
Academy Award, 45
Academy Awards, 135
Academy of Theatrical Arts, 11
Actors' Trade Union, 26
Alcohol and drugs, 105, 127, 130, 132, 148, 156, 157, 158, 159
Allan, Elizabeth, 124
Ameche, Don, 120
America, 3, 17, 21, 23, 120, 139
American
    cinema, 139
    Film Institute, 119
    film studios, 98
    filmmakers, 21
    filmmaking, 17
    Indians, 4, 5, 6
    stage, 35, 48
Ames, Leon, 109, 110
Anatol, 13
Ankers, Evelyn, 139, 142
Arabesque, 33
Arch, Lillian, 115, 155
Arisztid, 17
Armadillos, 69
Armand, 121
Armandi, 28
Arsenic and Old Lace, 91
Ashbury Park, New Jersey, 38
Atkinson, Brook, 36
Atwill, Lionel, 124
Austria, Vienna, 13, 19, 20
Az Ordog, 12

B

B-films, 106, 132
Balcombe, Florence Ann Lemon, 46
Balderston, John, 34
Baritone, 10
Barnum and Bailey, 64
Baron Frankenstein, 83
Barron, Henry, 29, 30
Barrymore, Lionel, 124
Barton, Charles, 150
Bat, The, 36
Beast People, 118
Beaudine, William, 144
Beebe, Ford, 133
"Bela Logo", 5
Bela the Gypsie, 140
Bellamy,
    Madge, 111
    Ralph, 130
Benet, Felix Dr., 99
Berlin, Germany, 28, 121, 122
Betty Boop, 146
Biltmore, 38

B *continued*

Black
   Camel, The, 110
   Cat, The, 93, 94, 96, 98, 100
   Dragons, 136, 144-146
   Friday, 137, 138
   Sleep, The, 160, 161
Blasko, Bela, 2
Blood of Dracula, The, 48
Bodeen, DeWitt, 104
Body Snatcher, The, 103-105, 148
Bogdanovich, Peter, 91, 95
Borg, Reginald Le, 161
Borga Pass, 68
Boreland, Carroll, 77, 124, 125
Bow, Clara, 39, 40
Bowery at Night, 147
Bowery Boys, 143
Brackett, Charles, 134, 135
Brasov, 2
Brewster, Jonathan, 91
Bride of Frankenstein, 98, 100, 101
Bride of the Atom, 157
Bride of the Monster, 157
British
   Board of Censors, 98, 130, 131,
      134
   Count Dracula, 33
   International Pictures, 127
Broadminded, 110,
Broadway, 10, 29, 33, 35, 121
Broadway stage, 69
Brooks, Mel, 103
Brown, Joe E., 110
Browning,
   Charles Albert, 64
   Tod, 51, 63-66, 69, 73, 75, 76, 83,
      123, 124, 126
Budapest, 11, 13, 15, 18, 28, 114
Budapest Theater Society, The, 17
Bulgaria, 135
Burton, Tim, 105

C

Cabinet of Dr. Caligari, 74, 88

Cable, Clark, 115
"California Magyarsagi", 136
Calloway, Cab, 116
Canada, 90
Cappola, Francis Ford, 45
Captain Hook, 91
Carfax
   Abbey, 46, 47
   Art Gallery, 46
Carpathian Mountains, 1, 2, 14, 103
Carradine, John, 147, 149, 160
Casablanca, 17
Caspian Mountains, 68
Castle Dracula, 2, 68
Chan, Charlie, 110, 123
Chandler, Helen, 57
Chandu the Magician, 115, 116
Chaney
   Lon Jr., 140-143, 148-150, 160, 161
   Lon, 51, 63-66, 69, 70, 81, 109,
      126, 139
Chaplin, Charlie, 115
Christ, Jesus, 11
Clarence, O. B., 134
Clarens, Carlos, 97
Clive, Colin, 101
Cobwebs, 52, 68, 71
Cockneyed World, The, 110
Coffin, Tristan, 147
Colonel March, 91
Columbia Theater, 40
Communism, 17, 24, 40, 135, 137, 153,
   154
Communist Party, 16
Continental School, 35
Cooper, Willis, 101
Corbin, John, 29
Corpse Vanishes, The, 147
Costello, Lou, 150
Councits' Republic, 26
Count
   Alucard, 148, 149
   Dracula, 3, 14, 35-37, 41, 46, 48, 49,
      52-54, 57, 59, 60, 63, 64, 69, 78,
      110
Courtney, William, 63
Crawford, Joan, 116

Criminal Code, The, 91
"Cult Movies #3", 94
Curse of the Cat People, 104
Curtiz, Michael, 17, 18
Cyrano de Bergerac, 28

D

Daniell, Henry, 104, 105
Dark Eyes of London, 132, 133
De Voe, Daisy, 40
Dead Un-Dead, The, 45
Death Kiss, The, 116
Declaration for Immigration, 26
Depp, Johnny, 154
Der Januskopf, 21
Devil, 45
Devil in the Cheese, The, 33
Devil's in Love, 116
Divorce, 20, 31, 41, 155
Doctor
    Dearborn, 134
    Frankentstein, 83
    Mirakle, 108, 110
    Moreau, 119,
Doumont (French fortress), 95
Doyle, Conan, 51
Dr. Jekyll and Mr. Hyde, 21, 146
Dracula, 10, 16, 20, 21, 33-42, 45-50,
    52, 54-57, 59-62, 65-75, 77, 81, 82,
    86, 88, 90, 96, 100-102, 107, 108,
    110, 111, 116, 123, 127, 129, 131,
    134, 163
Dracula, 1, 2, 3, 5, 45, 116, 117, 120,
    121, 148, 149, 157, 160, 161
Dracula's Daughter, 129
"drug and alcohol free", 159
Dublin Mail, The, 44
Dublin, Ireland, 44
Duchess Sophie, 14
Dumb Girl of Portici, The, 90
Dwan, Alan, 132
Dworkin, Andrea 46

E

East Side Kids, 143, 144

Edinburgh, Scotland, 104
Elizabeth, 83
England, 95, 127, 136, 139
English, 26, 30, 31, 101, 105, 106
"Europe's most romantic stage
    actor", 11
Europe, 4, 9, 12, 16, 92, 130, 136
European stage, 11, 20
Exorcist, The 38
Eyes, 5, 27, 39, 69, 75, 77, 112, 116,
    141
Ez Ember, 72

F

"Father of American Filmmaking", 64
Federal Bureau of Investigation, 154
Feldman, Marty, 103
Female vampire, 16, 52
Ferdinand, Archduke Francis, 13
Fernando, 29
Fifty Million Frenchmen, 42, 110
Filmograph Magazine, 70, 71, 73
Films of Bela Lugosi, 77
First
    American film, 32
    film, 20
    horror-sound film, 73
    Hungarian Literary Society, 26
    National Pictures, 42
Florey, Robert, 82-84, 88, 110
Flynn, Emmett, 42
Ford, Wallace, 123
Fox Pictures, 30, 31, 42, 115, 132, 133
Fox, Sidney, 109, 110
Frankenstein, 8, 82, 85-89, 91, 92, 96,
    100, 107-110, 117
Frankenstein Meets the Wolf Man,
    104
Frankenstein, 129, 141
Frankenstein, Dr., 82-84
Freaks, 66
Free Organization of Theater Em-
    ployees, 17
Freund, Karl, 21, 27, 67, 69, 70, 68, 69
Friday-the-thirteenth, 75
Friedlander, Louis, 97

f *continued*

Frye, Dwight, 68, 88, 101
Fulton Theater, 35-37, 39

G

Gangs, 4, 6
Garbo, Greta, 116, 132, 134, 135
Gecko, 11
German
    cinema, 20, 23, 28
    film community, 23
Germans, 2
Germany, 95, 101, 103
Ghost
    of Frankenstein, 92, 139
    Ship, 104
Ghosts On the Loose, 143, 144
Glen or Glenda, 154, 155, 157
Glimpy, 144
Golden Era, 64, 73, 106
Goldwyn, Samuel, 21
Golem, 95
Gorilla, The, 132
Gothic romance, 45
Great Britain, 48, 98, 103, 130, 132
Great White Way, 30
Greenwich Village Theater, 29, 30
Griffith, Corrine, 42
Griffith, D. W. 51, 64
Gypsies, 3, 6

H

Hall,
    Albert 70
    Doctor Many, 138, 139
    Huntz, 144
    Mordaunt, 48
Halliwell, Leslie, 93, 110, 138
Halliwell's Film Guide, 93, 110, 138
Halparin Brothers (Victor and
    Edward), 110, 111
Harker,
    Jonathan, 47, 68
    Lucy, 38, 39

Hersholt, Jean, 124
Hisston, 31
Hollywood, 3, 4, 15, 21, 31, 39, 52, 54,
    64, 73, 76, 82, 84, 87, 89, 92, 94,
    101, 105, 113, 115, 117, 122-124,
    126, 150, 154, 158, 162
Hollywood Hills, 129
Hollywood on Parade, 116
Holmes, Sherlock, 52
Holy Cross Cemetery, 164
*Horror: A Connoisseur's Guide to
    Literature and Film*, 114, 118
Horthy, Miklos, 18
House Committee on Un-American
    Activities, 153, 154
House of Frankenstein, 150
House of Pain, 118
Howe, James Wong, 124
Hungarian
    Army, 15
    filmmaking, 17
    Literary Society, 25
    Repertory Company, 28, 26
    stage, 8, 10
Hungary, 2-4, 7, 8, 14, 16-18, 20, 55,
    93, 120, 121, 137
Huntley, Raymond, 33, 34, 41
Hutchinson, Josephine, 103

I

"I am Dracula", 10, 67, 69, 70
I Walked With A Zombie, 104
Industrial Light and Magic, 140
International House, 116
Invisible Ghost, The, 146
Invisible Man, The, 89
Invisible Ray, The, 99, 100, 133
Island of Doctor Moreau, The, 87,
    117
Island of the Lost Souls, 116-119, 147

J

Japan, 145, 146
Jeno, Istvan, 12
Jolly, Sanford, 146

Joseph I, Emperor Francis, 13
Jukes, Bernard, 39
Juliet, 13

K

Kalamy, Bela, 13, 81-106, 117, 122, 137, 138, 164
Karolyi, Count Michael, 18
Katzman, Sam, 138
KBS Films, 116
Keeper of Men, 87
Keith, Carlos, 104
Keith, Ian, 63
KFI Radio, 61, 86
King Kong, 119
King of Horror, 65, 92, 97
Korda, Alexander, 18

L

Laemmle, Carl, 82, 87-90, 100, 101, 107, 108
Lake Elisnore, 155
Landau, Martin, 154
Las Vegas, Nevada, 53, 115
Lasko,
    Bela, 7
    Istvan, 3, 6, 8
    Joanna, 3
    Ludovious, 3
    Paula Vojnits, 3, 8
    Vilma, 3, 8, 9
"Latin Lover", 78
Laughton, Charles, 87, 118, 119
Le Borg, Reginald, 140, 161
Lee
    Christopher, 77
    Rowland V., 101, 102
Legend, 7, 42
Leipard, The, 17
Lengyel, Melchar, 135
Leventon, Vladimir, 104
Lewton, Val, 103-105
Lexington Theater, 29
Lighting, 5
Lininger, Hope, 160

Lithuania, 135
Liveright, Horace, 34-36, 61
Living Hypnotic Corpse, 64
Lon Chaney Sr., 100
London After Midnight, 124
London, 48, 70
Lone Ranger, 145
Long Beach News, 129
Lorre, Peter, 132, 137
Los Angeles, California, 38, 61
Los Angeles General Hospital, 158
Lost Island, The, 87
Lost Patrol, The, 91
"Love the Actor", 18
Lubin, Arthur, 138
Lubitsch, Ernst, 134
Lugos, Hungary 2, 3, 6, 7, 10, 13
Lugosi,
    Bela Jr. 132, 155
    Dezso, 10
Lukas, Paul, 18

M

Mai Szinlap, 12
Maleva, 153
Man of a Thousand Faces, 64
Manfred, 28
Manners, David, 57, 68-70, 116
Maria, 84
Mark of the Vampire, 77, 123, 124-127
Marmont, Percy, 109
Mason, Dr. Tom, 162
Master of Macabre, 9, 92, 109, 123, 139, 142, 164
McCarthy hearings, 137, 153
Meeks, Donald, 124,
Mescall, John, 96
Metro-Goldwyn-Mayer, 42, 48, 66, 104, 123, 124, 126
Metropolitan State Hospital, 158
Mexico, 135
Meyrinck, Gustav, 95
Mickey Mouse, 146
Midnight Girl, The, 32, 33
Modern Screen, 72, 130

continued

Mohr, Karl, 28
Monogram Pictures, 104, 122, 138, 143, 145, 146
Moore, Clayton, 145
Moore, Roger, 136
Morning Telegraph, 141
Moscow, Russia, 135
Mother Goose, 91
Motherland, 7, 16, 21
Motion Picture Museum and Hall of Fame, 116
Motion Picture Relief Fund, 131, 132
Mrs. Frankenstein, 103
Mssrs. McLaglen and Lowe, 110
Mummy, The, 87, 100
Muni, Paul, 63
Murder Legendre, 115, 116
Murders in the Rue Morgue, 88, 108, 109, 110, 111
Murnau, F. W., 20
Mute, 9
Mute valet, 161
Mysterious Mr. Wong, The, 122
Mystery of Mary Celeste, The, 127

N

Nagybanyhegyes, Ilona Montaugh de, 21, 28, 30, 31
National Theater of Hungary, 12, 16, 28, 114, 121
Neuwald Brothers, 136
New Haven, Connecticut 35
New York, 35, 55, 63, 122
    Telegraph, The, 42
    Times, The 36, 48, 84
New York City, New York, 25, 28, 31, 32, 39, 76
Night of Terror, 116
Night of the Living Dead, 110
Ninotchka, 134, 135, 136
Norwalk, California, 158
Nosferatu The Vampire, 21

Oakland, Simon, 148
Oh, For A Man, 42
Old Mother Riley Meets the Vampire, 153
Open House, 34
Orloff, 134
Ouspenskaya, Maria, 153

P

Panama, 32
Paramount Pictures, 104
Parson, Louella, 131
Pasternak, Joseph, 4
Pathe Film, Ltd., 133
Pavlovs, Anna, 90
Peary, Danny, 94
"Peeping Tom", 83
Pembroke, George, 145
Peter Pan, 91
Peterson, Dorothy, 38, 39
Phantom Creeps, The, 132, 133
Phantom of the Opera, The 34, 70, 74, 100, 163
Philadelphia Public Ledger, 7
Photos, 5, 27, 65, 71, 85, 125, 149, 163
Pickford, Mary, 116
Pierce, Jack, 87, 88, 91, 141, 142
Plan 9 From Outer Space, 154, 161
Poe, Edger Allan, 93-95, 97, 98, 108, 109
"poetry in motion", 123
"poverty row", 130
Pratt, William Henry, 90
PRC Studios, 104
Prince, 121
Princess Saratoff, 30
Princip, Gavrilo, 13, 14
Prisoners, 42
Punch and Judy, 83

Radium X, 100
Raines, Claude, 89, 142, 143

Rathbone, Basil, 160, 161
Raven, The, 97, 98
Red Poppy, The, 29-31
Reefer Madness, 116
Reefer Man, 116
Reish, Walter, 135
Renfield, 39, 68, 67
Resita, 7, 8, 9, 10
Return of Chandu, The, 6
Ringling Brother's Circus, 64
Ritz Brothers, 132
RKO Studios, 103, 104, 160
Road to Mandalay, The, 51
Robson, Mark, 104
Rocky Mountains, 68
Romania, 1, 2, 4
Romeo and Juliet, 7
Romeo, 12, 13, 28, 127
Romero, George, 110
Ross, Robert, 46
Roxy Theater, 75, 76
Rukh, Janus, 99
Rumania, 139
Russell, Elizabeth, 147
Russia, 14

S

"Safe-house", 24
Saint, 136
Saints Double Trouble, The, 136
San Francisco Chronicle, 41
San Francisco, California, 40, 41
Sanders, George, 136
Sarajevo, 14
Saratoff, Princess, 30
Satan, 81, 97
Sayer of the Law, 117
"scalpers", 4
Scalps, 6, 7
Schnitler, Arthur, 13
Scotland Yard, 91, 103
Screen Actors Guild, 120
Seitzer, William, 42
Selznick, David O., 104
Sex symbol, 11, 15
Shakespeare, William, 7, 11, 12

Shelley, Mary Wollstonecraft, 82, 107
Sheriff, R. C., 84
Shirley, Lillian, 72
Silent Command, The, 31, 32
Silent film, 32
Sills, Milton, 135
Silver Star, 14
Sklaven Femdes Willens (Slave of a Foreign Will), 20
Small, Edward, 31
Son of Dracula, 148, 149, 150, 161
Son of Frankenstein, 100-103
Sophie, Duchess, 14
Spooks Run Wild, 143, 144
Star Film Company, 17
Stevenson, Robert Louis, 21, 103
Stoker,
Bram, 21, 43, 46, 47, 55, 63, 66, 77, 86
Mrs. Florence (Bram), 21, 34, 46, 47
Strickfaden, Kenny, 89
Superior Hungarian State Gymnasium, 6
Szabados, Zoltan, 136, 137,
Szeged, 11, 13
Szineszek Lapsa, 19
Szinhaz es Mori Ojsag, 34
Szmik, Ilona, 15, 20

T

Talbot, Larry, 140
Tamiroff, Akim, 160
Targets, 91
Technicolor, 101
Tell, William, 28
Tepes, Vlad, 44
Terror of Transylvania, 1
The Chain of Destiny, 44
"the evilest man in Hollywood", 92
The New York Times, 29
Thirteenth Chair, The, 42, 66
Thriller, 91
Tisza, Count Stevan (Italian freighter), 23, 24, 25

T *continued*

To-Day's Cinema, 41
Tourner, Jaques, 104
Tradgedy Man, The, 29
Transylvania, 1, 46, 52, 64, 139
Transylvanian Count, 148
Trilby, 11
Tuttlew, Bill, 124
Typecast, 32, 77

 U

Ulmer, Edger, 93, 95
Under Two Flags, 51
Unholy Three, The, 51
United Artists, 160
Universal
    City, 53
    Pictures, 3, 48, 50, 51, 58, 61-65,
       68, 70, 75, 76, 100, 107, 130,
       138, 143
    Studios, 5, 26, 73, 75, 86, 91, 97,
       104, 125, 149, 149, 163
Unknown, The, 51
Unveiled Woman, The, 42

 V

Valentine's Day 1931, 75
Valentino, Rudolph, 115
Vampire, 43, 45, 81, 96, 150
Vampires, 47, 49, 53, 55, 56, 126
Vampires Over London, 153
Van Helsing, Dr., 39, 48, 50, 59, 78, 90
Van Sloan, Edward, 39, 48, 50, 59, 69,
    78, 90, 116
Veldt, Conrad, 63
Victor, 83
Virgin of Stamboul, The, 51
Vlad Dracula, 1, 2
Vlad the Impaler, 1, 64, 68
Vollin, Doctor, 97, 98
Voodoo Man, 147

W

Ward, David, 155

Ware, Judge William Wallace L., 158
Warner Brothers, 42
Waycoff, Leon, 109
Webber, Andrew LLoyd, 34
Weeks, Beatrice, 40
Wells, H. G., 87, 117
Werewolf, The, 33
West, Dorothy, 113, 114
Whale, James, 83, 84, 89
Which Woman, 51
Whirl of Mirth, The, 51
Whispering Shadow, The, 116
White Zombie, 110, 111, 115, 147
Wilde, Oscar, 46
Wilder, Billy, 134
*Willard and King's Great Traveling
    Show*, 51
Williams, Jean D., 34
Winwood, Estelle, 29, 30
Wise, Robert, 104
Wives, 15, 20, 21, 28, 40, 115, 155, 160
Wolf Man, The, 3, 33, 87, 138-140,
    142, 143, 153
Wolf, Leonard, 115, 118
Women of All Nations, 110
Wood,
    Ed Jr., 105, 154, 155, 157, 159, 162
    Representative John, 153
World War I, 93, 95
World War II, 14, 145

 Y

Yellow Films, 122, 123
Yellow Lily, 121
Ygor, 101, 102, 103
Yohalem, George, 123
You'll Find Out, 137
Young Frankenstein, 103
Yugoslavia, 135